PROTECTING PERSONAL INFORMATION

The concept of privacy has long been confused and incoherent. The right to privacy has been applied promiscuously to an alarmingly wide-ranging assortment of issues including free speech, political consent, abortion, contraception, sexual preference, noise, discrimination and pornography. The conventional definition of privacy, and attempts to evolve a 'privacy-as-a-fence' approach, are unable to deal effectively with the technological advances that have significantly altered the way information is collected, stored and communicated. Social media platforms such as Facebook pose searching questions about the use and protection of personal information and reveal the limits of conceiving the right to privacy as synonymous with data protection. The recent European Union's GDPR seeks to enforce greater protection of personal information, but the overlap with privacy has further obscured its core meaning. This book traces these troubling developments, and seeks to reveal the essential nature of privacy and, critically, what privacy is not.

Protecting Personal Information

The Right to Privacy Reconsidered

Andrea Monti
and
Raymond Wacks

·HART·
OXFORD · LONDON · NEW YORK · NEW DELHI · SYDNEY

HART PUBLISHING
Bloomsbury Publishing Plc
Kemp House, Chawley Park, Cumnor Hill, Oxford, OX2 9PH, UK

HART PUBLISHING, the Hart/Stag logo, BLOOMSBURY and the Diana logo are
trademarks of Bloomsbury Publishing Plc
First published in Great Britain 2019

First published in hardback, 2019
Paperback edition, 2020

A catalogue record for this book is available from the British Library.

Library of Congress Cataloging-in-Publication Data

Names: Monti, Andrea, 1967- | Wacks, Raymond, author.

Title: Protecting personal information : the right to privacy reconsidered /
Andrea Monti & Raymond Wacks.

Description: Oxford, UK ; Chicago, Illinois : Hart Publishing, 2019. |
Includes bibliographical references and index.

Identifiers: LCCN 2019004742 (print) | LCCN 2019006640 (ebook) |
ISBN 9781509924868 (EPub) | ISBN 9781509924851 (hardback)

Subjects: LCSH: Data protection—Law and legislation. | Privacy, Right of.

Classification: LCC K3560 (ebook) | LCC K3560 .M66 2019 (print) | DDC 342.08/58—dc23

LC record available at https://lccn.loc.gov/2019004742

ISBN: HB: 978-1-50992-485-1
PB: 978-1-50994-616-7
ePDF: 978-1-50992-487-5
ePub: 978-1-50992-486-8

Typeset by Compuscript Ltd, Shannon

To find out more about our authors and books visit www.hartpublishing.co.uk. Here you will find
extracts, author information, details of forthcoming events and the option to sign up for our newsletters.

To Alessia, Penelope, Gea, and Nicolò

PREFACE

Common parlance and literature are replete with references to 'privacy' in both its physical and metaphysical sense. Characters in novels are forever invading each other's 'privacy' by a host of unsolicited acts and practices. While these colloquial and literary usages convey an often appealing representation of an intrusion into an individual's private life, their inevitable insinuation into the law has, unhappily, impaired the concept's meaning and hindered the positive evolution of a well-defined right to privacy.

The working title of this book was *What Privacy is Not*. Exasperated by the application of the notion of 'privacy' to an ever-expanding number of harms, we set out to identify the underlying anxiety at the heart of apprehensions about this fundamental right.

Our uneasiness rests not simply on dissatisfaction with terminological or linguistic imprecision, but also on the loose application of 'privacy', especially in the United States, to a diverse array of subjects ranging from abortion, contraception and sexual preference to pornography, and even noise. This misguided approach has entered Europe and the European Union where the overlap between privacy and data protection has caused needless obfuscation.

If 'privacy' is to be effectively protected by the law, certainty and clarity are required. These qualities are lacking in what has become a confused and often incoherent muddle. Our task is to eliminate, as far as possible, the ambiguity and imprecision that has plagued this important right for too long. The failure to recognise – ideally by carefully drafted legislation – the right to privacy is a major source of this predicament.

We offer an alternative to this liberally expansive interpretation. While we do not disparage or reject the numerous sociological and philosophical examinations of privacy, our quest is to identify the core interest that warrants legal protection, and to suggest how – as a matter of law – it can best be safeguarded and defended.

Wielding a form of Occam's razor, we hope to show that the nucleus of a viable legal concept of privacy is the protection of personal information. Moreover, we detect an increasing acceptance that this is indeed the correct approach; that privacy is best conceived as an interest in protecting an individual's personal information. Surely when we condemn the attacks on our privacy we lament the loss of control over intimate facts about ourselves. Is the quintessence of that control not the exercise of control over our most sensitive details, whether they be pried upon or wantonly circulated?

As lawyers of different legal cultures, we have inevitably drawn, where appropriate or useful, on the experience of our respective jurisdictions, but we hope that our analysis transcends any particular legal system. Indeed, we have resisted the temptation to focus too sharply on the legislative or judicial practice of any single legal system, selecting instead judgments from a range of countries.

In the ensuing pages we attempt to demonstrate the cause of the current conceptual confusion, its adverse effects, and how it might best be eradicated. Recognising privacy as a legal right is a crucial first step. By enacting specific legislation or constitutional provision, the right to privacy is transformed from a philosophical or sociological notion. We acknowledge, of course, that this positivist solution is no panacea, but unless the right is to languish in its current fog of uncertainty and ambiguity, there is no workable alternative.

Privacy is a fundamental right, but we do, of course, acknowledge the importance of other rights that are central to any democratic society, some of which, like freedom of expression, are conceived as competing with individual privacy.

We are indebted to Sinead Moloney, Roberta Bassi, Rosamund Jubber and Tom Adams of Hart Publishing for their cheerful assistance in steering this work through its various stages. Thanks too to our exceptional copy editor, Jo Choulerton.

Andrea Monti
Raymond Wacks

ACKNOWLEDGEMENTS

I wish to record my (always inadequate) profound debt to the late Giancarlo Livraghi. He was a friend, a mentor, a passionate champion of human rights, and a giant of the international advertising world. More than 20 years ago he recruited me into ALCEI, the first NGO outside the US to fight for digital rights and we continued the struggle until his sad demise in 2014. Though he has gone, his works live on.

I want also to thank Professor Giampiero Di Plinio. As a scholar of public law, he understood decades ago, much earlier than others, the importance of studying the relationship between technology and the Constitution, and supported my entering the academic community.

As always, there are countless friends that I must thank. Paolo Nuti, Stephen Firth, Stefano Chiccarelli, Pierluigi Perri, Enrico Zimuel, Axel Spies, Luca Luparia, Giuseppe Gennari, Francesco Perna, Maurizio Codogno, Andrea Cocito, Marco Cappato, Stefano Zanero, Hiroshi Miyashita, Andrea Paolini, and Manlio Cammarata are a few among many who, by their academic, professional or political involvement, have contributed to sustaining privacy as a fundamental right.

Andrea Monti

I am deeply indebted to an ensemble of colleagues, commissioners, and cognoscenti for their encouragement, advice, and assistance over the years. They include Michelle Ainsworth, John Bacon-Shone, Eric Barendt, Colin Bennett, Paul Bernal, Jon Bing, the late Peter Birks, Michael Bryan, Ann Cavoukian, the late 'Con' Conway, Alex Flach, David Flaherty, Graham Greenleaf, Godfrey Kan, Justice Michael Kirby, Stephen Lau, Robin McLeish, Mr Justice Barry Mortimer, Helen Nissenbaum, Charles Raab, Megan Richardson, Geoffrey Robertson QC, the late Stefano Rodotà, Joshua Rozenberg QC, Jamie Smith QC, Hugh Tomlinson QC, and Nigel Waters. None necessarily endorses the approach adopted in this work.

I have been privileged sporadically to descend the ivory tower to serve on law reform and other bodies dedicated to exploring the complex idea of privacy, and drafting proposals to protect this fundamental right. I am grateful to the members of the Law Reform Commission of Hong Kong privacy sub-committee from whom I learned so much.

Raymond Wacks

CONTENTS

TABLE OF CASES

European Union

Australia

Canada

Finland

France

Germany

Hong Kong

India

Italy

Japan

United States

TABLE OF LEGISLATION

Directives

1

Personal Information and Privacy

The traffic in data is at the heart of our digital world. The recent Facebook controversies are merely one instance of the extent to which personal information has become the lifeblood of modern technology. It is self-evident that our 'privacy' is threatened by the relentless advances in a host of intrusive activities that includes surveillance, genetics, biometrics, GPS, and anti-terrorist measures. The torrent of private information online as a consequence of the intensification of blogs, social networking sites, Twitter, and other devices of the information age continues unabated. And the appetite for gossip and 24-hour rolling news generates ever-greater sensationalism and 'fake news'.

The Internet spawns risks that were inconceivable even 20 years ago. The methods by which data are collected, stored, exchanged and used have been transformed, and consequently so has the nature of the threats to 'privacy'. At the same time, traditional cultural activities such as photojournalism and the preservation of our collective memory are threatened by a notion of privacy that is both distorted and excessively expanded.

The quotation marks around 'privacy' are intentional. We hope to establish that the use of this popular term, though entirely appropriate as a general description of the interest that warrants protection, is irrevocably nebulous, and fails to provide – for legal purposes – an adequately precise definition of the concern that cries out for effective protection.[1]

In the ensuing chapters we attempt to show why the law ought to eschew the many conceptual and doctrinal ambiguities of 'privacy', by recognising that it is the protection of personal information which is at the core of our disquiet about the increasing frailty of this essential value. The law must therefore concentrate its efforts on the protection of personal information, which we define to include

---

[1] For previous attempts to demonstrate this failure, see R Wacks, *Personal Information: Privacy and the Law* (Oxford: Clarendon Press, 1989 and 1993); R Wacks, 'The Poverty of "Privacy"' (1980) 96 *Law Quarterly Review* 73; R Wacks, 'Privacy Reconceived: Protecting Personal Information in a Digital World' in Eli Lederman and Ron Shapira (eds), *Law, Information and Information Technology* (The Hague: Kluwer Law International, Law and Electronic Commerce series, 2001) 75–97; R Wacks, 'What has Data Protection to do with Privacy?' (2000) 6 *Privacy Law and Policy Reporter* 143, R Wacks, 'Privacy in Cyberspace: Personal Information, Free Speech, and the Internet' in Peter Birks (ed), *Privacy and Loyalty* (Oxford: Clarendon Press, 1997) 93–112; R Wacks, *Privacy and Media Freedom* (Oxford: Oxford University Press, 2013); R Wacks, *Law, Morality, and the Private Domain* (Hong Kong: Hong Kong University Press, 2000), Part Two.

those facts, communications or opinions which relate to an individual and which it would be reasonable to expect him or her to regard as intimate or sensitive and therefore to want to withhold, or at least to restrict their collection, use, or publication. 'Facts' are, of course, not restricted to textual data, but embrace a wide range of data that can be extracted from numerous sources including images and DNA, as well as from technologies that make available other genetic and biometric data from fingerprints, face and iris recognition, and the ever-increasing types of information about us that technology is able to reveal, use, and misuse by analysing (or purporting to analyse) our behaviour in both its exterior appearance and internal origins.

It is the control of personal information that is central to any workable legal conception of the right to privacy.

Attempts to devise neutral and instrumental definitions of privacy overlook the fundamental concerns that lie at the heart of any meaningful concept of privacy. So, for example, to argue that it is a 'myth' that privacy only matters in relation to critically sensitive, important information and not for trivial, mundane or 'unimportant' information or 'low value' correspondence[2] is to drain privacy of its significance and deny its claim to legal protection as a right beyond that provided by data protection legislation (which regards personal information as any information about an individual).

It may be objected that perfect clarity is never attainable, or that the interpretive skills of judges obviate the need for impeccable precision. But, as we hope to demonstrate, the imprecision that attends the law's treatment of 'privacy' not only generates misunderstanding and ambiguity, but contributes to the adulteration of this fundamental right. Like software coding, difficulties arise when the same variable is assigned different values; the software will not work. Similarly, the law – and, in particular, the recognition and enforcement of a legal right – is undermined by vague or unduly capacious language.

This is the unfortunate fate of the legal concept of 'privacy', which has developed into an umbrella word whose sprawling scope weakens its protection. To inflate rights is often to devalue them. Privacy has grown into a meta-concept that extends beyond its legal formulation. For instance, the title of Article 8 of the European Convention on Human Rights (ECHR) reads 'Right to respect for private and family life' while Article 7 of the Charter of Fundamental Rights of the European Union (hereafter EU Charter) is similarly entitled 'Respect for private and family life'. Yet, curiously, the EU Directive 95/46 (Protection of Personal Data) Article 1 declares:

> In accordance with this Directive, Member States shall protect the fundamental rights and freedoms of natural persons, and in particular their *right to privacy* with respect to the processing of personal data (emphasis added).

---

[2] Paul Bernal, *The Internet, Warts and All: Free Speech, Privacy and Truth* (Cambridge Intellectual Property and Information Law) (Kindle Location 5782) (Cambridge: Cambridge University Press, 2018, Kindle Edition).

In other words, the Directive [now superseded by the General Data Protection Regulation (GDPR)] seeks to protect a right (the right to privacy) that is absent from the EU Charter of Fundamental Rights!

Article 8 of the ECHR reads:

Right to respect for private and family life

1. Everyone has the right to respect for his private and family life, his home and his correspondence.

2. There shall be no interference by a public authority with the exercise of this right except such as is in accordance with the law and is necessary in a democratic society in the interests of national security, public safety or the economic well-being of the country, for the prevention of disorder or crime, for the protection of health or morals, or for the protection of the rights and freedoms of others.

The notion of 'private and family life' is excessively wide. What could reasonably lie outside it? My 'private life' is, in effect, my existence, my being.[3] This provision is as ambiguous and indeterminate as the 'right to be let alone' that Warren and Brandeis invoked to describe the right to privacy in their celebrated essay,[4] which, as discussed below, is the principal source of the confusion and incoherence.

Nor does Article 8 protect 'privacy' *stricto sensu*. Indeed, if it protects 'privacy' at all, it protects the right to '*respect*' for privacy. Disconcertingly, the European Court of Human Rights has construed it to include 'physical and psychological integrity',[5] protection of one's environment,[6] identity,[7] and personal autonomy.[8] The reach of the notion of 'private life' contained in Article 8, thus extends well beyond the putative protection of privacy, let alone personal information.

The situation is no better in the United States, which evinces the same 'Baron Münchhausen bootstrapping' state of affairs.[9] While there are statutes that proclaim 'privacy' in their title, such as the Privacy Act of 1974,[10] the term does not appear in the United States Constitution. The foundation for a good deal of privacy protection is the Fourth Amendment which safeguards 'The right of the

---

[3] Notwithstanding this expansive and nebulous phrase, the European Court of Human Rights has sporadically ruled against an applicant: in *Botta v Italy* Application 21439/93, (1998) 26 EHRR 241, the Court rejected a claim that the failure to provide disabled persons with adequate physical access to a beach violated Article 8.

[4] Samuel D Warren and Louis D Brandeis, 'The Right to Privacy' (1890) 4 *Harvard Law Review* 193, 196.

[5] *YF v Turkey* Application 24209/94, (2004) 39 EHRR 34, [33]; *Pretty v United Kingdom* Application No 2346/02, (2002) 35 EHRR 1 61].

[6] *Hatton v United Kingdom* Application No 36022/97, (2003) 37 EHRR 28, [119], including the right to sleep.

[7] *Pretty v United Kingdom* Application No 2346/02, (2002) 35 EHRR 1, [61].

[8] *Goodwin v United Kingdom* Application No 28957/95, (2002) 35 EHRR 523, [90].

[9] Actually, the fictional character created in 1785 by German writer Rudolf Erich Raspe lifted himself by pulling his pigtail and not his bootstraps. Nevertheless he has become the symbol of one who attempts an impossible self-executing task.

[10] Privacy Act of 1974 (5 USCA 552a).

people to be secure in their persons, houses, papers, and effects, against unreasonable searches and seizures'.[11]

It is worth mentioning that the German Constitutional Court has 'discovered' a new basic right in the German Basic Law; citizens have a 'fundamental right to the confidentiality and the integrity of information technology systems'.[12]

Furthermore, the situation has been rendered even more vexing by the advent of data protection law and regulation which, as will become evident in the next chapter, is increasingly regarded as synonymous with privacy.

In this book, we offer an alternative analysis. We seek to demonstrate what privacy is *not*; to illustrate that many of the purported instances of privacy-related conditions or claims should be excluded from any practical legal conception of the right. By eliminating these mistaken applications of privacy to the specific conduct or activities described, what remains ought to provide a more accurate concept of privacy and, we trust, a more effective means by which to protect this fundamental right.[13]

While technology is re-shaping traditional legal concepts, an often neglected factor is the impact of the social networking platforms on both the creation of a new right and the meaning of a traditional right. The networking ability of individuals is available to anyone who can operate a smartphone. User-generated content and social networking sites enhance the capacity to engineer social, political, and legal change. The fate of 'privacy' protection is no less susceptible to these developments. For example, we contend that 'photo/socio-journalism', also known as 'street-photography' (documenting slices of life by candid pictures), does not

---

[11] Other Amendments have also been deployed by the Supreme Court in its quest to protect 'privacy', including the First, Ninth, and Fourteenth Amendments. The 1993 Russian constitution does not include a specific section on the right of privacy, but merely mentions the word 'тайну' in Articles 23 and 29. But 'тайну' can be translated in various ways, with different nuances ranging from 'privacy' to 'secret'. Neither the Italian, nor the French or German constitutions contain a word that easily fits within the vague 'privacy' definition – and the same can be said for many other countries. This is chiefly because 'privacy' is an English word and national legal systems are expressed in their national languages that can contain similar – or perhaps the same – ideas but formalised in a different way, with different words. The Constitution of South Africa includes, in Section 14, the protection of the right to privacy. The shortcomings of both its phraseology and judicial interpretation are briefly canvassed in Chapter 8 of this volume.

[12] Federal Constitutional Court judgment of 27 February 2008: 1 BvR 370/07, 1 BvR 595/07, BVerfGE 120, 274. According to the Federal Constitutional Court, the general right to privacy ('informational self-determination') arising from Article 2(1) in conjunction with Article 1(1) of the Basic Law also includes a fundamental right to ensure the confidentiality and integrity of information technology systems.

[13] See, for an example of a similar approach, the dictum of Supreme Court Justice Potter Stewart: 'I shall not today attempt further to define the kinds of material I understand to be embraced within that shorthand … and perhaps I could never succeed in intelligibly doing so. But I know it when I see it.' *Jacobellis v Ohio*, 378 US 184 (1964); https://supreme.justia.com/cases/federal/us/378/184/. At a more abstract level, 'privacy' is similar to the Kantian noumenon, a 'legal idea in itself' therefore not directly knowable except in its phenomenal perception as constructed by the chaotic turbulence of the interaction among media, politics and social behaviour made possible by the (now) ubiquitous use of the Internet.

infringe 'privacy': see Chapter six. Nor is 'privacy' necessarily violated when a court, following exacting legal procedures, permits the law enforcement authority to eavesdrop upon the suspect's communications.

We do not therefore offer a taxonomy of the different meanings assigned to 'privacy'. This subject has, of course, provided a fertile field of research for philosophers, social scientists, and lawyers. And we resist the temptation to examine or question the immense literature that continues to emerge at a fairly alarming rate. Our purpose is different. We refrain from taking issue with the countless scholars that have contributed to this seemingly interminable debate. Instead we want to improve the legal protection of the information we most value and cherish. By safeguarding sensitive or intimate information, we defend a fundamental right that vouchsafes our individual freedom and personal identity.

I. The Genesis

Hailed as 'the outstanding example of the influence of legal periodicals upon American law'[14] the famous article of 1890 gave birth to the legal recognition of privacy in the United States. Written by Samuel D Warren and Louis D Brandeis, their commentary was published in the influential *Harvard Law Review*.[15] The two lawyers, Warren, a Boston attorney and socialite, and Brandeis, who would be appointed to the Supreme Court in 1916, incensed by the original paparazzi and so-called 'yellow journalism', wrote what is often characterised as the most influential law review article ever published.[16]

Their essay denounced the press for their impudence, and contended that their conduct constituted an invasion of their privacy the right to which, they claimed, was inherent in the common law. Drawing upon decisions of the English courts relating to, in particular, breach of confidence, property, copyright, and defamation, they maintained that these cases were merely instances and applications of a general right to privacy, of the 'right to be let alone.' The common law, they asserted, although under different forms, protected an individual whose privacy

---

[14] WL Prosser, 'Privacy' (1960) 48 *California Law Review* 383.

[15] SD Warren and LD Brandeis, 'The Right to Privacy' (1890) 4 *Harvard Law Review* 193; See, too, WF Pratt, 'The Warren and Brandeis Argument for a Right to Privacy' (1975) *Public Law* 161; H Kalven, 'Privacy in Tort Law: Were Warren and Brandeis Wrong?' (1966) 31 *Law & Contemporary Problems* 326; DL Zimmerman, 'Requiem for a Heavyweight: A Farewell to Warren and Brandeis's Privacy Tort' (1983) 68 *Cornell Law Review* 297. This section draws on parts of Chapter 3 of R Wacks, *Privacy and Media Freedom* (Oxford: Oxford University Press, 2013).

[16] The essay 'enjoys the unique distinction of having theoretically outlined a new field of jurisprudence': D Larremore, 'The Law of Privacy' (1912) 12 *Columbia Law Review* 693. It is usually claimed that the catalyst for their annoyance was that the press had spied on Warren's daughter's wedding. But this is improbable since, in 1890, she was six years old! The more likely source of their anger was a series of articles in a Boston high-society gossip magazine, describing Warren's stylish dinner parties.

was invaded by snooping. In so doing the law recognised the significance of the spiritual and intellectual needs of man. They declared:

> The intensity and complexity of life, attendant upon advancing civilization, have rendered necessary some retreat from the world, and man, under the refining influence of culture, has become more sensitive to publicity so that solitude and privacy have become more essential to the individual; but modern enterprise and invention have, through invasion upon his privacy, subjected him to mental pain and distress, far greater than could be inflicted by mere bodily injury.[17]

The common law, they reasoned, has developed from the protection of the physical person and corporeal property to the protection of the individual's '[t]houghts, emotions and sensations'.[18] But as a result of threats to privacy from recent inventions and business methods and from the press, the common law needed to go further. An individual's right to determine the extent to which his thoughts, emotions, and sensations were communicated to others was already legally protected but only in respect of authors of literary and artistic compositions and letters, who could forbid their unauthorised publication. And though English cases recognising this right were based on protection of property, in reality they were an acknowledgement of privacy, of 'inviolate personality'.[19]

It did not take long before their thesis was tested in court. The plaintiff complained that her image had been used without her consent to advertise the defendant's merchandise. She was portrayed on bags of flour with the dire pun, 'Flour of the family'. A majority of the New York Court of Appeals rejected the Warren and Brandeis opinion, ruling that the privacy argument had 'not as yet an abiding place in our jurisprudence, and … cannot now be incorporated without doing violence to settled principles of law'.[20] The minority, however, was persuaded; Gray J declaring that the plaintiff had a right to be protected against the use of her image for the defendant's commercial advantage: 'Any other principle of decision … is as repugnant to equity as it is shocking to reason.'[21]

The decision was not popular[22] and led to the enactment by the State of New York of a statute rendering unlawful the unauthorised use of an individual's name or image for advertising or trade purposes.[23] A mere three years later in a case involving similar facts, the Supreme Court of Georgia approved of the judgment of Gray J.[24] The Warren and Brandeis argument, 15 years after its publication,

---

[17] Warren and Brandeis, n 15 above, 196.
[18] ibid, 195.
[19] ibid, 205.
[20] *Roberson v Rochester Folding Box Co* 171 NY 538, 64 NE 442 (1902) 447.
[21] ibid, 450.
[22] A criticism of the judgment by the *New York Times* seems to have been the cause of one of the majority judges taking the unusual step of defending the decision: O'Brien, 'The Right of Privacy' (1902) 2 *Columbia Law Review* 437.
[23] NY Sess Laws (1903) ch 132, paras 1–2, subsequently amended in 1921, NY Civil Rights Law, paras 50–51.
[24] *Pavesich v New England Life Ins Co*, 50 SE 68, 68 (Ga 1905).

had prevailed. Following that historic decision, most American States have incorporated the 'right to privacy' into their law.

Over the years the American common law continued to expand its protection of privacy. In 1960, Dean Prosser, a leading tort expert, expounded the view that the law now recognised not one tort, 'but a complex of four different interests … tied together by the common name, but otherwise [with] nothing in common.'[25] He outlined their nature as follows:

1. Intrusion upon the plaintiff's seclusion or solitude or into his private affairs.

The wrongful act consists in the intentional interference with the plaintiff's solitude or seclusion. It includes the physical intrusion into the plaintiff's premises, and eavesdropping (including electronic and photographic surveillance, 'bugging' and telephone-tapping). Three requirements must be satisfied:[26] (a) there must be actual prying (disturbing noises or bad manners will not suffice); (b) the intrusion must offend a reasonable man; and (c) it must be an intrusion into something private.

2. Public disclosure of embarrassing private facts about the plaintiff.

Three elements of the tort are indicated by Prosser: (a) there must be publicity (to disclose the facts to a small group of people would not suffice); (b) the facts disclosed must be private facts (publicity given to matters of public record is not tortious); and (c) the facts disclosed must be offensive to a reasonable man of ordinary sensibilities.

3. Publicity which places the plaintiff in a false light in the public eye.

According to Prosser,[27] this tort normally arises in circumstances in which some opinion or utterance (such as spurious books or views) is publicly attributed to the plaintiff, or where his picture is used to illustrate a book or article with which he has no reasonable connection. The overlap with the tort of defamation is at once apparent and, though the false light 'need not necessarily be a defamatory one',[28] it is submitted that an action for defamation will invariably lie in such cases. The publicity must be 'highly offensive to a reasonable person'.[29]

4. Appropriation, for the defendant's advantage, of the plaintiff's name or likeness.

Under the common law tort, the advantage derived by the defendant need not be a financial one;[30] it has, for instance, been held to arise where the plaintiff was

---

[25] WP Keeton, DB Dobbs, RE Keeton and DG Owen (eds), *Prosser & Keeton on, the Law of Torts*, 5th edn (St Paul MN, West Publishing Co, 1984) 855.

[26] *Prosser & Keeton*, n 25 above, 856–67; *Restatement*, para 652 D.

[27] *Prosser & Keeton*, n 25 above, 863–64; *Restatement*, para 652 E.

[28] ibid.

[29] *Restatement*, para 652E, comment b.

[30] *Prosser & Keeton*, n 25 above, 853; *Restatement*, para 652C, comment b.

wrongly named as father in a birth certificate. The statutory tort (which exists in several States) normally requires the unauthorised use of the plaintiff's identity for commercial (usually advertising) purposes; the New York statute,[31] upon which most of the current legislation is modelled, confines itself to advertising or 'purposes of trade'.[32] The recognition of this tort establishes what has been called a 'right of publicity'[33] under which an individual is able to decide how he wishes to exploit his name or image commercially. It is difficult to see how the protection of this essentially proprietary interest is connected with the protection of even a general 'right to privacy'.[34] It is only the torts of 'intrusion' and 'public disclosure' that 'require the invasion of something secret, secluded or private pertaining to the plaintiff'.[35] It might therefore be argued that the torts of 'appropriation' and 'false light' are not properly conceived of as aspects of 'privacy'.[36]

Some view this fourfold segregation as misconceived because it undermines the Warren and Brandeis axiom of 'inviolate personality' and neglects its moral basis as an aspect of human dignity.[37] The classification has nevertheless assumed a prominent place in American tort law, although, as anticipated by the jurist Harry Kalven, it has to a large extent ossified the conception into four types:

> [G]iven the legal mind's weakness for neat labels and categories and given the deserved Prosser prestige, it is a safe prediction that the fourfold view will come to dominate whatever thinking is done about the right of privacy in the future.[38]

The vicissitudes of these four torts have been charted in a gargantuan welter of academic and popular literature.[39] Almost every advanced legal system has, to a greater or lesser extent, sought to recognise various aspects of privacy, not always with clarity or consistency.[40]

---

[31] New York Civil Rights Law 1921, Titles 50–51.

[32] This has been widely defined; see eg, *Spahn v Julian Messner, Inc* 23 App Div 2d 216; 260 NYS 2d 451 (1964).

[33] MB Nimmer, 'The Right of Publicity' (1954) 19 *Law and Contemporary Problems* 203; Kalven, n 15 above, 331.

[34] See RC Post, 'Rereading Warren and Brandeis: Privacy, Property, and Appropriation' (1991) 41 *Case Western Reserve Law Review* 647.

[35] *Prosser & Keeton*, n 25 above, 814.

[36] 'Its splendid pedigree notwithstanding, false light has proved in practice to illuminate nothing. From the viewpoint of coherent first amendment theory, it has served to deepen the darkness', DL Zimmerman, 'False Light Invasion of Privacy: The Light that Failed' (1989) 64 *New York University Law Review* 364, 453.

[37] EJ Bloustein, 'Privacy as an Aspect of Human Dignity: An Answer to Dean Prosser' (1964) 39 *New York University Law Review* 962.

[38] H Kalven, 'Privacy in Tort Law: Were Warren and Brandeis Wrong?' (1966) 31 *Law & Contemporary Problems* 326, 332.

[39] Several of the most significant – and influential – articles may be found in R Wacks (ed), *Privacy*. Vol I: *The Concept of Privacy*; Vol II: *Privacy and the Law*, The International Library of Essays in Law and Legal Theory (London/Dartmouth/New York: New York University Press, 1993).

[40] They include Austria, Canada, China, Taiwan, Denmark, Estonia, France, Germany, Holland, Hungary, Ireland, India, Italy, Lithuania, New Zealand, Norway, the Philippines, Russia, South Africa, South Korea, Spain, Thailand, and the majority of Latin American countries.

II. Defining 'Privacy'

A satisfactory definition of privacy continues to elude commentators. Alan Westin famously treats privacy as a claim: the 'claim of individuals, groups, or institutions to determine for themselves when, how, and to what extent information about them is communicated to others.'[41] But this miscarries as a definition since it includes the use or disclosure of *any* information about an individual. Moreover, an association of privacy with what might be called naked or general control means that we lose privacy when we are prevented from exercising control, even if, for some reason, we are unable to disclose personal information. Similarly, when we voluntarily disclose personal information, do we really lose our privacy? We are exercising rather than relinquishing control.

In short, this sense of naked control fails adequately to describe privacy; for while we may have control over whether to disclose information, it may, of course, be acquired by other means. If, however, control is meant in a stronger sense (namely that to disclose information, even voluntarily, constitutes a loss of control because we have lost the means to restrain the broadcasting of the information by others), it describes the potential for, rather than the actual, loss of privacy.

In other words, treating privacy as broad-spectrum control (or autonomy), assumes that it concerns our freedom to choose privacy. But, as pointed out, we may choose to abandon our privacy; in such a case a control-based definition relates to the question of the nature of our choices rather than the manner in they are exercised.

Another approach is to describe the characteristics of privacy itself. But this is always contentious. One perspective is that privacy consists of 'limited accessibility': a cluster of three related but independent components: *secrecy* – information known about an individual; *anonymity* – attention paid to an individual; and *solitude* – physical access to an individual.[42] It claims that we lose our privacy when others obtain information about us, or pay attention or gain access, to us. This analysis is said to possess four advantages. First, it is neutral, providing an objective identification of a loss of privacy. Secondly, it exhibits the coherence of privacy as a value. Thirdly, by identifying the invasions warranting legal protection, it demonstrates the utility of the concept in legal contexts. Finally, it includes 'typical' violations of privacy and eliminates those issues which, as argued above, although often regarded as privacy questions, are best viewed as moral or legal issues in their own right (noise, odours, prohibition of abortion, contraception, homosexuality, and so on).

However, even this perceptive analysis is problematic. In its pursuit of a neutral definition of privacy, it rejects definitions that are based on the attributes of the information involved, as presented in these pages; namely that the core of the

---

[41] Alan F Westin, *Privacy and Freedom* (New York: Atheneum, 1967) 7.
[42] Ruth Gavison, 'Privacy and the Limits of Law' (1980) 89 *Yale Law Journal* 412.

concept and the right to privacy is the use or misuse of information that is 'private' in the sense of being intimate or related to the individual's identity. If a loss of privacy occurs whenever *any* information about us becomes known (the secrecy component), the notion is significantly attenuated. It is a contortion to describe *every* instance of the unsolicited use of information as a loss of privacy. Some limiting or controlling factor is required. The most acceptable factor is arguably that the information be 'personal'. To maintain that whenever we are the subject of attention or when access to us is obtained we necessarily lose privacy is to strip our anxiety about our privacy of an important part of its significance. Being the subject of attention or being subjected to uninvited intrusions upon your solitude are offensive in their own right, but our concern about privacy in these situations is strongest when we are conducting activities which we would typically regard as private.

A further difficulty is that disputes about the meaning of privacy are advanced from essentially dissimilar premises. For example, when privacy is described as a 'right', issue is not really joined with those who regard it as a 'condition'. The former is generally a normative statement about the need for privacy (however defined), while the latter is merely a descriptive statement about 'privacy'. Furthermore, assertions about the attraction of privacy tend to confuse its instrumental and inherent value: privacy is considered by some as an end in itself, while others perceive it as a means by which to safeguard other social ends such as creativity, love, or emotional release.

Yet another contention is that by defending the values underlying privacy (property rights, human dignity, protection against discrimination or against the infliction of emotional distress, and so on), we might obviate the need to debate the legal protection of privacy. This reductionist position seriously weakens the conceptual distinctiveness of privacy.

III. Privacy and Personal Information

The alternative proposed here is, without adulterating the importance of privacy as a fundamental right, to identify the specific problems that generate our apprehensions. While the original archetypal complaints concerned what the American law calls 'public disclosure of private facts' and 'intrusion upon an individual's seclusion, solitude or private affairs',[43] contemporary anxieties naturally relate to the collection and misuse of computerised personal data and metadata, and other issues associated with our digital society. They share the need to limit the degree to which private facts about us are published, intruded upon, or generally misused.

---

[43] See section II above.

The approach advanced in these pages gives rise to two basic questions. First, what is 'personal' and, secondly, under what conditions is a subject to be regarded as 'personal'? Is a matter 'personal' by virtue merely of the assertion that it is so, or are there matters that are inherently personal? To declare that our political views are personal is contingent upon certain norms which forbid or restrict queries into, or unapproved accounts of, such opinions. It may, however, suffice to invoke the norm that entitles us to keep our views to ourselves. These norms are obviously culture-relative as well as mutable. There is unquestionably less reticence in most modern communities with regard to several aspects of private life than characterised societies of even 50 years ago. The age of social media has dramatically transformed attitudes towards revealing the most intimate facts.

Any definition of 'personal information' must include both the nature of the information and the wish to control it. The notion of 'personal information' is therefore both descriptive and normative. Personal information includes those facts, communications, or opinions which relate to us and which it is reasonable to expect we would consider intimate or sensitive, and therefore want to withhold, or at least to control access to them or their collection, use, or circulation.

'Facts', as mentioned, are not, of course, confined to textual data, but encompass a wide range of information, including those extracted from images, DNA, and other genetic and biometric data such as fingerprints, face and iris recognition, and the constantly growing categories of information about us that technology is able to reveal and exploit.

IV. A Constitutional Right

For some time these four torts endured as the primary means by which the American law protected privacy in different forms. They were also, more or less, the boundaries of the constitutional protection of privacy. The main concern of Warren and Brandeis was, of course, what we would now call media intrusion. In 1928 Justice Brandeis (as he had then become) dissented forcefully in the case of *Olmstead v United States*.[44] He declared that the Constitution conferred 'as against the Government, the right to be let alone', adding, '[t]o protect that right, every unjustifiable intrusion by the Government upon the privacy of the individual, whatever the means employed, must be deemed a violation of the Fourth Amendment.'[45] That view was adopted by the Supreme Court in *Katz v United States*.[46] Since then privacy as the right to be let alone has been invoked by the Court in this context.

---

[44] *Olmstead v United States* 277 US 438 (1928).
[45] ibid, 473.
[46] *Katz v United States* 398 US 347 (1967).

The most momentous – and contentious – development came in 1965 with the Supreme Court's decision in *Griswold v Connecticut*.[47] It declared unconstitutional a Connecticut statute prohibiting the use of contraceptives because it violated the right of marital privacy, a right 'older than the Bill of Rights'.[48]

Although the word 'privacy' appears nowhere in the Constitution, in a succession of cases the Supreme Court has – via the Bill of Rights (particularly the First, Third, Fourth, Fifth, and Ninth Amendments to the Constitution therein) recognised, amongst other privacy rights, that of associational privacy,[49] 'political privacy',[50] and 'privacy of counsel'.[51] It has also set the limits of protection against eavesdropping and unlawful searches.[52]

By far the most divisive 'privacy' decision that the Court has decided is the case of *Roe v Wade* in 1973.[53] It held by a majority, that the abortion law of Texas was unconstitutional as a violation of the right to privacy. Under that law abortion was criminalised, except when performed to save the pregnant woman's life. The Court held that States may prohibit abortion to protect the life of the foetus only in the third trimester. The judgment, which has been described as 'undoubtedly the best-known case the United States Supreme Court has ever decided',[54] is simultaneously embraced by feminists and deplored by many Christians. It is the slender thread by which the right of American women to a lawful abortion hangs. There appears to be no middle ground. Ronald Dworkin, describes the vehemence of the dispute:

> The war between anti-abortion groups and their opponents is America's new version of the terrible seventeenth-century European civil wars of religion. Opposing armies march down streets or pack themselves into protests at abortion clinics, courthouses, and the White House, screaming at and spitting on and loathing one another. Abortion is tearing America apart.[55]

No less intense a tempest was created by *Bowers v Hardwick* in 1986 in which a bare majority held that the privacy protections of the due process clause did not extend to homosexual acts between consenting adults in private: 'No connection between family, marriage, or procreation on the one hand and homosexual conduct on the other has been demonstrated.'[56] This decision was explicitly overruled in *Lawrence v Texas* in which, by six to three, the Supreme Court decided

---

[47] *Griswold v Connecticut* 381 US 479 (1965).

[48] ibid 486.

[49] *National Association for the Advancement of Colored People v Alabama* 357 US 449 (1958).

[50] *Sweezy v New Hampshire* 364 US 234 (1957).

[51] *Massiah v United States* 377 US 201 (1964).

[52] *Olmstead v United States* 277 US 438 (1928); *Goldman v United States* 316 US 129 (1942).

[53] *Roe v Wade* 410 US 113 (1973). See too *Planned Parenthood v Casey* 505 US 833 (1992).

[54] Ronald Dworkin, *Life's Dominion: An Argument about Abortion and Euthanasia* (London: Harper Collins, 1993) 4.

[55] ibid, 103.

[56] *Bowers v Hardwick* 478 US 186 (1986) 284.

that it had construed the liberty interest too narrowly. The majority held that substantive due process under the Fourteenth Amendment entailed the freedom to engage in intimate consensual sexual conduct.[57] Its effect is to nullify all legislation throughout the United States that purports to criminalise sodomy between contenting same-sex adults in private.

The American experience is instructive. Other common law jurisdictions continue to wrestle with the stubborn difficulties of definition, scope, and the balancing of privacy with other competing rights, particularly freedom of expression. In general, the approach of the common law is largely interest-based, while the continental tradition of civil law jurisdictions tends to be rights-based. In other words, while the English law, for example, adopts a pragmatic case-by-case approach to the protection of privacy, French law conceives privacy as a fundamental human right. This difference has nonetheless been tempered by the impact of the European Convention on Human Rights and other declarations and Directives emanating from Brussels.

V. A Way Forward

If imprecision has impeded the effective legal recognition of 'privacy', how should we proceed? The recognition of a legal right to privacy (notwithstanding the confusion the concept engenders) has a 'collateral' benefit: it assists in bringing closer together the divergent approaches of the common and civil law systems. In respect of the former, the words of Lord Hoffmann still resonate:[58]

> There seems to me a great difference between identifying privacy as a value which underlies the existence of a rule of law (and may point the direction in which the law should develop) and privacy as a principle of law in itself. The English common law is familiar with the notion of underlying values – principles only in the broadest sense – which direct its development. A famous example is ... freedom of speech [as an] ... underlying value ... But no one has suggested that freedom of speech is in itself a legal principle which is capable of sufficient definition to enable one to deduce specific rules to be applied in concrete cases. That is not the way the common law works.[59]

---

[57] *Lawrence v Texas* 539 US 558 (2003).

[58] *Wainwright v Home Office* [2003] UKHL 53, [31] per Lord Hoffmann.

[59] 'Au contraire', would be Warren and Brandeis' response. Their case for the legal recognition of the right of privacy was the precise opposite. They reasoned that the common law had developed from the protection of the physical person and corporeal property to include the protection of the individual's '[t]houghts, emotions and sensations': SD Warren and LD Brandeis, 'The Right to Privacy' (1890) 4 *Harvard Law Review* 193, 195. An individual's right to determine the extent to which these were communicated to others was already legally protected, but only in respect of authors of literary and artistic compositions and letters who could forbid their unauthorized publication. And though English cases recognizing this right were based on protection of property, in reality they were an acknowledgement of privacy, of 'inviolate personality' (ibid, 205).

From a civil law perspective, however, the acknowledgement of the existence of a 'new' right can occur only by way of a complex and delicate exercise in legal interpretation. While this is, of course, possible, and has to some extent been achieved by the English courts in their interpretation of the Human Rights Act 1998, a clearly drafted statute is manifestly preferable.[60] A draft bill is proposed in the Appendix.

It is, of course, impossible to avoid using 'privacy' to describe the right that warrants legal protection. Indeed, it makes perfect sense to speak of 'privacy' as shorthand for the individual and social interest[61] that we champion. But, in pursuit of effective safeguards, the vagueness that besets the term is best eschewed. Our uneasiness is founded not simply on semantics, but also on the unrestrained application of 'privacy' to a diverse collection of subjects from abortion, contraception and sexual preference to noise and pornography. The quest is not for conceptual purity, but legal certainty.

To invoke 'privacy' as if it were a talisman endowed with magical power is an imperfect, and potentially negative, manner by which to deliver legal certainty. '[T]he cardinal principle', declares HLA Hart, '[is] that legal words can only be elucidated by considering the conditions under which statements in which they have their characteristic use are true.'[62] In other words, it is mistaken to believe that, from a legal standpoint, the idea of 'privacy' or 'private life' can be usefully applied without a careful enquiry into the specific conduct or interests lying beneath claims for its protection.

There have, of course, been many such attempts, and the literature is awash with sociological, philosophical, legal and other explorations of the matter. The argument presented here does not seek to address, let alone disparage or repudiate, these scholarly endeavours, but it considers that, by generally adopting a broad conception of 'privacy' they tend to discount the critical question of the control over personal information that lies at the heart of our anxieties. By perceiving the

---

[60] An interpretive approach is central to Ronald Dworkin's theory of law. See, especially, *Taking Rights Seriously* (London: Duckworth, 1978) and in *A Matter of Principle* (Cambridge MA: Harvard University Press, 1985), *Law's Empire* (Cambridge MA: Harvard University Press, 1986), and *Justice in Robes* (Cambridge MA/London: Harvard University Press, 2006). For an outline of Dworkin's theory see Raymond Wacks, *Understanding Jurisprudence: An Introduction to Legal Theory*, 5th edn (Oxford: Oxford University Press, 2017) Chapter 5.

[61] Charles Raab, 'Privacy, Social Values and the Public Interest' in A Busch and J Hofmann (eds), *Politik und die Regulierung von Information* (*Politische Vierteljahresschrift*, Sonderheft 46, Baden-Baden: Nomos verlagsgesellschaft, 2012) 129–51: Kirsty Hughes, 'A Behavioural Understanding of Privacy and its Implications for Privacy Law' (2012) 75 *Modern Law Review* 806.

[62] See HLA Hart, 'Definition and Theory in Jurisprudence' (1954) 70 *Law Quarterly Review* 37 in HLA Hart, *Essays in Jurisprudence and Philosophy* (Oxford: Clarendon Press, 1983), Essay 1, p 47. This 'makes it vital to attend to Bentham's warning that we should not ... abstract words like "right" ... from the sentences in which alone their full function can be seen, and then demand of them so abstracted their genus and differentia' (ibid, 31). See too R Birmingham, 'Hart's Definition and Theory in Jurisprudence Again' (1984) 16 *Connecticut Law Review* 774 for an illuminating account of Frege's analysis, which includes his view that law is plausibly a scientific discourse and that sentences, not words, are the unit of meaning.

subject in this manner, the core of the value is diminished or lost altogether. Except as an abstract description of its underlying meaning or social, political, or philosophical significance, until an actual legal right is recognised, the term 'privacy' (though colloquially unavoidable) should be avoided as a cause of action. This, we believe, is the soundest foundation upon which to base effective *legal* protection of this fundamental right and restrict the notion to matters that relate to 'privacy' properly so called.

While it is heartening that the jurisprudence has affirmed the existence of an independent right, its conceptual foundation is far from clear. The notion of 'private life' is unfortunately as nebulous as Warren and Brandeis' vague 'right to be let alone'.[63] And the European Court of Human Rights appears to be satisfied that it should be so. Thus, to take only one instance, it held that Article 8 protects the right to sleep.[64] Should this, undeniably vital, interest be regarded as a human right? As argued above, the very concept of 'private life' invites obscurity and abstraction. This is plain from an early decision of the Court, that declared:

> [T]he right to respect for private life does not end [at the right to privacy, ie, the right to live, as far as one wishes, protected from publicity]. It comprises also, to a certain degree, the right to establish and to develop relationships with other human beings, especially in the emotional field for the development and fulfilment of one's own personality.[65]

Is this not an unmistakeable endorsement of the vast reach of Article 8? 'We cannot', it has been justly remarked, 'inflate the concept of human rights so much that it covers the whole realm of justice. Human rights would lose their distinctive moral force.'[66] This is not to deny the significance of individual rights or even their formulation in broad terms, which facilitates their recognition by the law; however, as one American commentator has stated, 'a natural "right" to privacy is simply inconceivable as a legal right – sanctioned perhaps by society but clearly not enforceable by government ... Privacy itself is beyond the scope of law.'[67]

---

[63] See R Wacks, 'The Poverty of "Privacy"' (1980) 96 *Law Quarterly Review* 73. See too H Kalven, 'Privacy in Tort Law: Were Warren and Brandeis Wrong?' (1966) 31 *Law & Contemporary Problems* 326.

[64] See, for example, the decision in *Hatton v United Kingdom* Application 36022/97, (2002) 34 EHRR 37, which accepted the proposition that sleep disturbance, distress, and illness caused by night flights at Heathrow airport could constitute a violation of the claimants' right to private life under Article 8 of the ECHR.

[65] *X v Iceland* Application 6825/74, (1976) 5 DR 86, 87.

[66] G Letsas, *A Theory of Interpretation of the European Convention on Human Rights* (Oxford: Oxford University Press, 2007) 25. It is part of our argument that the unremitting exercise of human rights inflation has devalued the currency. As James Griffin puts it, '[t]he term "human right" is nearly criterionless. There are unusually few criteria for determining when the term is used correctly and when incorrectly – not just among politicians, but among philosophers, political theorists, and jurisprudents as well. The language of human rights has, in this way, become debased.' J Griffin, *On Human Rights* (Oxford: Oxford University Press, 2008) 14–15.

[67] RF Hixson, *Privacy in a Public Society: Human Rights in Conflict* (New York/Oxford: Oxford University Press, 1987) 98.

The effect of decisions such as this is to extricate 'privacy' from its habitat as a legal concept, and implant it into a moral or ethical realm thereby weakening its claims as a legal right. When the law comes to recognise such a right, we are forced back to square one since the moral right will stand in need of legal definition and application.

VI. Personal Information

Nothing in our approach contradicts the need to evaluate the context in which personal information arises. When considering whether the information in question satisfies the threshold requirement of 'personal', the facts that are the subject of the individual's complaint will naturally need to be examined 'in the round'. Publicly accessible data (telephone numbers, addresses, number plates, and so on) cannot be regarded as data whose disclosure or circulation it is reasonable to seek to control or restrict. But when these data are rendered sensitive by their linkage to other data, a justifiable complaint may be said to arise.

Is a right to privacy required in order to address this issue? Data protection legislation would seem to be adequate. This matter is considered in the following chapter; suffice it to say here that data protection regulation applies only to data that is subject to automated processing, or by way of a filing system.

This does not entirely eliminate the influence of individual idiosyncrasy where its effect would be relevant to the circumstances of the case. Nor would an objective test negate the relevance of such elements in deciding whether it is reasonable for an individual to consider information as personal. The British, for example, are notoriously diffident about revealing their salaries. Scandinavians are far less reserved in this respect. Cultural factors unavoidably affect whether it is reasonable to consider information as personal.

No single item of information is – in and of itself – personal. An anonymous medical file, bank statement, or lurid disclosures of a sexual affair are innocuous until linked to an identified individual. Once the identity of the subject of the information is exposed it becomes personal. And once this threshold is crossed what is now personal information is worthy of protection only when it satisfies an objective test. But this does not occur in a conceptual or social vacuum; it must be evaluated by reference to the specific conditions under which disclosure is threatened or, more usually, made.

The promiscuous extension of the notion to 'decisional' matters (abortion, contraception, sexual preference), and its – understandable – conflation with freedom and autonomy, is a conceptual error. Fortunately, there appears to be a growing recognition that these (important) issues concern the exercise of freedom or autonomy, albeit in private. But 'private' or 'personal' in this context describes the fact that such decisions are normatively best left to the individual rather than the state. They are, in other words, private rather than public.

For legal purposes the meaning of 'privacy' corresponds to our intuitive under-standing of it as, fundamentally, our interest in protecting personal information. When we lament its erosion, we mourn the loss of control over intimate facts about ourselves.

It will at once be enquired why should different rights of 'privacy' be so char-acterised? And why can they not co-exist as diverse, but related, dimensions of the same essential conception? The answer, as already mentioned above, is not that we deny the importance of rights or even their expression in wide terms, which promotes their legal recognition. Rather it is based on the conviction that by addressing the problem as the protection of personal information, the persistent problems that are commonly pushed into the straitjacket of 'privacy' might more successfully be resolved.

The concepts of 'privacy' and 'private life' have become too vague and inco-herent to achieve the purpose of protecting our personal information.[68] This ambiguity has, as already argued, undermined the importance of this value and frustrated its effective protection. It has grown into as nebulous a notion as 'free-dom' (with which it is not infrequently equated) or 'autonomy' (with which it is regularly confused).[69] Furthermore, it endangers the development of a satisfactory theory of privacy. The more voluminous the concept, the less likely is its coherent conceptual expression.

It might be objected that the early, generous 'right to be let alone' essayed by Warren and Brandeis could easily accommodate a wide range of supposed privacy-invading conduct. But it is only by the most convoluted reasoning that the collection, processing, or misuse of personal data (let alone – in this Facebook age – the many forms of online exploitation and abuse), can be adequately encap-sulated within even so bountiful a mantra.

The elaborate attempt by Daniel Solove to conceive a 'taxonomy of privacy' is founded on the idea that we abandon the search for a common denominator or essence of privacy. Instead, he proposes that privacy be can usefully concep-tualised in terms of Wittgenstein's notion of 'family resemblances': although certain concepts might not share one common characteristic, they might form a 'network of similarities overlapping and criss-crossing.' Solove therefore proposes that instead of seeking an overarching concept of 'privacy', we ought to focus on specific forms of interference or disruption. But, on what basis, then, do certain practices constitute *privacy*-invading conduct if there is no shared concept of 'privacy'? The core idea of 'family resemblance' seems to invite the very elusiveness that Solove is at pains to avoid. His meticulous analysis produces an admirable theory of *infringement* of privacy, rather than of privacy itself, confirming the view

---

[68] An early expression of these difficulties is F Davis, 'What Do We Mean by "Right to Privacy"?' (1959) 4 *South Dakota Law Review* 1.

[69] For an attempt to derive the right to privacy from the 'moral principle ... of respect for indi-vidual liberty', see RB Hallborg, 'Principles of Liberty and the Right to Privacy' (1986) 5 *Law and Philosophy* 175.

that the concept is intractably incoherent.[70] Secondly, even among those who deny the parasitical character of 'privacy', there is little agreement concerning its principal defining features.

The following chapters will attempt to expose how 'privacy' has developed into a conceptual incubus in a number of areas. The confusion between privacy and data protection is a conspicuous example of the failure to elucidate the crux of privacy. The European Court of Human Rights increasingly applies the notion of privacy to activities conducted in public spaces. Moreover, the data protection authorities of many jurisdictions frequently conceive data protection as a synonym for the protection of private life, confusing the 'need-to-know' as a legal basis to access personal information, on the one hand, with the right to restrict that access, on the other.

Minorities invoke privacy as a legal basis on which to challenge discrimination. Politicians frequently claim privacy protection to shield their immoral behaviour. High-tech companies deploy privacy as a justification to design services that both make it difficult to co-operate with courts and lawyers and limit tort liability. There is also a growing techno-centric approach to privacy which tends to shift the debate away from the central legal and constitutional questions that are at the heart of its effective recognition and protection.

In what follows we trace these unsettling developments, and seek to reveal the essential nature of privacy and – critically – what the right to privacy is *not*.

---

[70] See DJ Solove, *Understanding Privacy* (Cambridge MA: Harvard University Press, 2008). But 'context' can be taken too far. See Helen Nissenbaum, *Privacy in Context: Technology, Policy, and the Integrity of Social Life* (Stanford CA: Stanford Law Books, 2009).

2

Personal Information
and Data Protection

I. Introduction

The anxiety generated in the 1960s by the advent of information technology evoked a call for regulatory and legal control over the collection and use of personal data. The German State of Hesse was the first to enact data protection legislation in 1970. This was followed by statutes in Sweden in 1973, the United States the following year, West Germany in 1977, and France in 1978.

The early 1980s saw two significant international instruments: the 1980 Organisation for Economic Co-operation and Development's Guidelines Governing the Protection of Privacy and Transborder Flows of Personal Data, and the 1981 Council of Europe's Convention for the Protection of Individuals with regard to the Automatic Processing of Personal Data. They contained explicit norms in respect of the process of handling electronic data. They emphasised, in particular, the need for the consent of the individual before personal data were collected.

These documents enunciated explicit rules governing the complete process of managing electronic data. At the core of data protection legislation, since the OECD guidelines, is the proposition that data relating to an identifiable individual should not be collected in the absence of a genuine purpose and the consent of the individual concerned. At a slightly higher level of abstraction, it encapsulates the principle of what the German Constitutional Court has called 'informational self-determination' – an ideal that expresses a fundamental democratic ideal.

Adherence to or, more specifically, enforcement of, this objective (and the associated rights of access and correction) has been mixed in the 40 or so jurisdictions that have enacted data protection legislation. Most of these statutes draw on the two international instruments mentioned above. Article 1 of the Council of Europe's Convention on the Protection of Individuals with Regard to Automatic Processing of Personal Data states that its purpose is:

> to secure in the territory of each Party for every individual, whatever his nationality or residence, respect for his rights and fundamental freedoms, and in particular his right to privacy, with regard to automatic processing of personal data relating to him ('data protection').

The importance of these principles cannot be exaggerated. In particular, the use-limitation and purpose-specification principles are crucial canons of fair information practice. Together with the principle that personal data shall be collected by means that are fair and lawful, they provide a framework for safeguarding the use, disclosure, and fair collection of such data. Personal data may be used or disclosed only for the purposes for which the data were collected or for some directly related purposes, unless the data subject consents. This key precept goes a long way towards regulating the misuse of personal data on the Internet. But it requires rejuvenation where it already exists and urgent adoption where it does so only partially (most conspicuously in the United States).

II. The Association of Data Protection and Privacy

While, at first blush, there would seem to be a substantial overlap between the objectives of data protection legislation, on the one hand, and the legal protection – legislative and judicial – on the other, the two should be kept analytically discrete. This is despite the fact that the language of the various papers, proposals, reports, regulations, and legislation frequently invoke the protection of 'privacy' as their purpose. So, for example, both the Committee established to formulate Britain's Data Protection Act 1984[1], and the Act itself, refer explicitly to 'privacy'. The former states that the statute was introduced for two main purposes, one of which was '[t]o counter the threat to privacy posed by the rapid growth in the use of computers, with their ability to process and link at high speed information about individuals'.[2]

This chapter attempts to show the important distinction between the two systems. It is, nevertheless, understandable why this conflation has occurred. Indeed, it might be asserted that the adoption of a data protection regime (appropriately modified) could provide an effective method by which to protect personal information.[3] For example, the focus of data protection regimes on the *processing* of personal data may render them better equipped both to anticipate and respond to the threats to privacy online caused by the ability to amass huge quantities of personal information. Secondly, they generally produce a practical and politically acceptable means by which personal data can be transferred across national boundaries. Thirdly, they avoid a good deal of the conceptual confusion of the 'privacy' discourse outlined in Chapter one.

---

[1] *Data Protection: the Government's Proposals for Legislation*, Cmnd 8539, April 1982.
[2] The paper, *Computers: Safeguards for Privacy* revisited the rules governing the storage and use of computerised information by Government departments. See http://researchbriefings.files.parliament.uk/documents/RP98-48/RP98-48.pdf.
[3] See Raymond Wacks, 'What has Data Protection to do with Privacy?' (2000) 6 *Privacy Law and Policy Reporter* 143.

Much of this addresses the 'right of privacy' and the attempts to 'balance' it against ostensibly competing rights. This vagueness and incoherence have obstructed the satisfactory legal protection of the interests with which the right is concerned. Fourthly, the growing international acceptance of a data protection normative framework, as expressed most recently in the EU General Data Protection Regulation (GDPR) and the legislation of many jurisdictions, supports an approach that may easily be implemented by domestic legislation, although there is a high risk of fragmentation at a national level as a result of the space permitted to Member States to harmonise their domestic legislation with EU law.

Fifthly, the adoption of a data protection regime could prevent – through the application of the principles that personal data be collected only for specified, explicit and legitimate purposes, and that those purposes be adequate, relevant and not excessive – certain forms of privacy-invading conduct that are currently conducted with impunity, such as surveillance, the storage and analysis of data arising therefrom, and perhaps even the intrusive activities of the media. Sixthly it has the capacity to address the ex post facto analysis of retained data.

Seventhly, its strategy is pre-emptive and preventive, particularly in respect of media intrusion where specific codes of practice could be brought under the aegis of the data protection authorities instead of the usually unsatisfactory purview of media 'councils'. Eighthly, a regulatory regime offers an important framework for the formulation of privacy policy by privacy or information commissioners who are able also to monitor and resist the introduction of legislation and practices that are inimical to the protection of personal information. Ninthly, a regulatory regime provides an effective means by which consumers may resolve privacy problems without resorting to expensive and protracted litigation. Finally, a regulatory regime can reflect community standards rather than the interests of the market.

These 10 apparent attributes may, however, be met by several counter-arguments that expose the limitations of a data protection analysis in protecting personal information. First, unelaborated, the current form and scope of the data protection approach is unlikely to adequately deal with a number of forms of attack on personal information such as the public disclosure of private facts by the media, and surveillance and intrusion. As data protection legislation applies only to automated or filing-system-based processing, it cannot cover most of the 'instantaneous' threats posed by paparazzi, snoopers, or hackers. Moreover, since the news media are an essential feature of a democratic society, their (mis)conduct is subject to the jurisdiction of the ordinary courts, and should not be within the purview of data protection commissioners. The interception of communications clearly requires its own regulatory controls within the general framework of the administration of criminal justice. Secondly, the data protection approach is founded upon a regulatory regime which has not only failed to commend itself (at least in the private sector) to lawmakers in the United States, but whose efficacy is often questioned in those jurisdictions which have adopted it, especially in respect of transborder data flow, in the light of the difficulties of ensuring compliance by companies based abroad.

Thirdly, a data protection approach is unsuited to address the constitutional balancing of free speech and the misuse of personal information; this is better contested in the self-consciously legal forum generated by the conventional approach. Fourthly, victims may find the administrative remedies provided by a regulatory regime inadequate as compensation for the abuse of their personal information, especially since data protection authorities under the GDPR lack the power to award compensation for the damage arising from breaches of the regulation. Fifthly, such a regime normally safeguards only recorded accessible data which accounts for only a proportion of the personal information which warrants protection. Finally, the numerous exemptions and defences, particularly those permitting the collection and transfer of personal data by law enforcement authorities or justified by considerations of national security, erode protection, and need to be treated with substantial circumspection; they are, in any event, excluded from the reach of the GDPR.

III. EU Data Protection Law

Generally speaking, the concept of personal data under the EU legislation is related to the notion of identity. Even though there are a few subtle distinctions between the language of Article 2 of EU Directive 95/46, the Data Protection Directive and Article 4 of EU Regulation 679/2016, the GDPR, they do not alter this fundamental point: personal data is information that identifies an individual or renders an individual identifiable.[4] In other words, the principal concern of data protection is *data* rather than information of an essentially private or intimate nature. The latter is the focus of what is commonly regarded as the nucleus of the 'right to (or of) privacy'.

At the core of the EU approach is a set of provisions requiring compliance with duties regarding data integrity, data availability, need to know, and confidentiality. Of these four pillars, only the last is directly connected to the protection of personal information; the other three actually advance the precise opposite: allowing personal data to circulate (relatively) freely.

---

[4] The starting point of any data protection law is the concept of 'personal data' or, in some statutes, 'personal information'. Article 4(1) of the GDPR employs the following formulation: '[A]ny information relating to an identified or identifiable natural person ("data subject"); an identifiable natural person is one who can be identified, directly or indirectly, in particular by reference to an identifier such as a name, an identification number, location data, an online identifier or to one or more factors specific to the physical, physiological, genetic, mental, economic, cultural or social identity of that natural person.'

It is true that the special regime of particular data as defined by Article 9 of the GDPR[5] is meant to provide additional protection to personal data,[6] but, again, only in the limited domain of automated and filing-system processing.

Thus, while data protection affords incidental or adventitious protection to genuinely personal or private information, it is neither intended nor equipped to satisfy the claims that arise from conduct that violates individual 'privacy'. This is not, of course, to dismiss the utility of data protection legal and regulatory systems, which in several respects offer a pragmatic route out of the labyrinth of the conceptual ambiguities of the 'privacy' discourse. Moreover, they are an indispensable tool in a world in which information technology disintegrates national borders, and international traffic in personal data is a routine feature of commercial life. The protection afforded to personal data in Country A is, in a digital world, rendered nugatory when that data is retrieved on a computer in Country B in which there are no controls over its use. Hence, states with data protection laws frequently proscribe the transfer of data to countries that lack them. Thus the EU has, in one of its many directives, explicitly sought to annihilate these 'data heavens'. Without data protection legislation, countries risk being shut out of the rapidly expanding information business.

On 24 October 1995 the European Parliament and the Council of Europe passed Directive 95/46 on the protection of personal data. This marked a significant recognition of the challenges posed by both the technological developments in the data processing sector and their application, which extends well beyond the typical scientific fields where massive data processing has long been routine since the earliest days of electronic computing.[7]

The GDPR came into force on 25 May 2018, superseding the Directive. As with the reports and statutes mentioned above, both the earlier Directive and the GDPR have widely been dubbed the 'Privacy Directive' and most national data protection authorities have called themselves a 'privacy authority'.[8] This has naturally induced a conflation between the two frames of reference. But, while the impetus for the Directive was the protection of personal data, its overriding objective was to regulate data bases or the automatic processing of personal information rather than to safeguard the general right of the individual to control personal

---

[5] Regulation (EU) 2016/679 of the European Parliament and of the Council of 27 April 2016 on the protection of natural persons with regard to the processing of personal data and on the free movement of such data, and repealing Directive 95/46/EC (General Data Protection Regulation) published OJ L119/1, 04/05/2016.

[6] This refers to 'sensitive data' of the now repealed EU Data Protection Directive, Directive 95/46/EC of the European Parliament and of the Council of 24 October 1995 on the protection of individuals with regard to the processing of personal data and on the free movement of such data, published OJ L281/31, 23/11/1995.

[7] In 1977 the US National Center for Atmospheric Research was the first officially to operate a Cray 1 supercomputer.

[8] For instance, as the *Whois* Server of the Italian Domain Registry shows, the domain 'garanteprivacy.it' was established by the Italian Data Protection Authority on 5 May 1999 and is still active and working (visited 17 March 2018).

(as in 'non-public') information whatever the means of collection, storage, or use. And this is the case notwithstanding the fact that Article 7 of the EU Charter of Fundamental Rights fails to distinguish between processed and 'non-processed' personal data.

The purpose of Directive 95/46 was clearly expressed. The fourth recital acknowledges that 'increasingly frequent recourse is being had in the Community to the processing of personal data in the various spheres of economic and social activity' and that 'the progress made in information technology is making the processing and exchange of such data considerably easier'.[9]

Article 3 of the Directive states explicitly the need for protection from the abuse of technology:

> This Directive shall apply to the processing of personal data wholly or partly by automatic means, and to the processing otherwise than by automatic means of personal data which form part of a filing system or are intended to form part of a filing system.

The Directive declares that its remit is the protection of fundamental rights and the right to privacy. But, as already mentioned, while this 'right to privacy' appears six times in the recitals[10] and twice in the Directive's articles,[11] the 'right to privacy' is nowhere to be found in the EU Charter of Fundamental Rights, whose Article 7 is related to the 'Respect for private and family life'. And while personal data protection is specifically addressed by Article 8 of the Charter, the Directive does not mention this provision. Furthermore, the other recitals[12] and articles[13] employ the term 'privacy' rather than 'right to privacy'.

Thus, if it is indeed the object of the Directive to protect the right to privacy, and yet there is no 'right to privacy' in the EU Charter (the closest instrument to a Constitution of the EU legal system) what exactly is the purpose of the Directive? Moreover, if the aim of the Directive is to protect – among other rights or interests – the right to privacy, what sort of right is the 'right to protection of personal data' protected by Article 8 of the EU Charter of Fundamental Rights? And if the right to the protection of personal data is instrumental in protecting the right to privacy, how is it possible that – from domestic data protection authorities down to the lower courts of Member States – data protection has become interchangeable with privacy?

Thus, even though the Data Protection Directive has ceased to be enforceable by the introduction of the GDPR, it remains necessary to take into account the corpus of interpretation and case law related to the notion of protection of personal data under the Directive itself that still flourishes.[14]

---

[9] Data Protection Directive, recital 4.

[10] Recitals 2, 7, 9, 10, 11, 68.

[11] Article 1 (Object of the Directive) and Article 9 (Processing of personal data and freedom of expression).

[12] Recitals 33 and 34.

[13] Article 12 (Right of access) and Article 26 (Derogation).

[14] 'The Regulation continues to follow the approach of the Data Protection Directive, but, building on twenty years of EU data protection legislation and relevant case law, it clarifies and modernises

It is plain that Article 8 of the EU Charter places the right to fair process-ing at the centre of the protection of personal data. Some of the attributes that follow from fair processing are identified by both the repealed Directive[15] and the GDPR,[16] such as the availability, authenticity, and integrity of personal data. These principles have nothing to do with respect for private life; on the contrary, one might claim that integrity and accuracy are actually the enemies of personal or intimate information. If personal data are *not* readily available and authentic, and lack integrity, profiling and mass surveillance are more difficult to accomplish. Nor it is easy for an intruder to assemble a dossier on an individual merely by accessing a single data source. In other words, it is hard to maintain the position that impos-ing these duties is related to the protection of 'privacy'.

To add confusion to contradiction, whereas the Directive employs the term 'privacy', the GDPR omits it altogether, referring instead to the EU Charter of Fundamental Rights, Article 7's 'respect for private and family life'. Indeed, the text of the GDPR puts beyond doubt that its paramount purpose is the technical one of processing personal data rather than the protection of the nebulous idea of 'privacy'.[17]

Another piece of EU legislation, namely, Directive 97/66,[18] and its successor, Directive 02/58[19] as amended by Directive 06/24[20] – which regulates 'the process-ing of personal data and the protection of privacy' in the telecommunications (the former) and electronic communication (the latter) sectors – deals with the relationship between personal data protection and privacy. As in the case of the Data Protection Directive, these have been, or will be, repealed[21] or amended.[22]

---

the data protection rules; it introduces a number of novel elements that strengthen the protection of individual rights and open opportunities for companies and business.' European Commission, Communication from the Commission to the European Parliament and the Council, 24 January 2018, COM(2018)43 *Stronger Protection, New Opportunities – Commission guidance on the direct application of the General Data Protection Regulation as of 25 May 2018*: http://eur-lex.europa.eu/legal-content/EN/TXT/HTML/?uri=CELEX:52018DC0043&from=en (visited 25 March 2018).

[15] Article 17 of the Data Protection Directive includes among the security measures to be adopted, the loss of protection (and then availability), alteration protection (and then integrity and authenticity.).

[16] GDPR recital 49.

[17] The GDPR completely drops the word 'privacy'; it appears only in a footnote of the recital 173, in reference to the Directive 2002/58/EC in favour of the wording of Article 8 of the European Conven-tion on Human Rights, and Article 7 of the EU Charter of Fundamental Rights (respect for private and family life). The latter is mentioned only once, in GDPR recital 4.

[18] Directive 97/66/EC of the European Parliament and of the Council of 15 December 1997 concerning the processing of personal data and the protection of privacy in the telecommunications sector – OJ L24, 30/01/1998.

[19] Directive 2002/58/EC of the European Parliament and of the Council of 12 July 2002 concern-ing the processing of personal data and the protection of privacy in the electronic communications sector – OJ L201, 31/07/2002.

[20] Directive 2006/24/EC of the European Parliament and of the Council on the retention of data generated or processed in connection with the provision of publicly available electronic communica-tions services or of public communications networks and amending Directive 2002/58/EC – OJ L105, 13/04/2006.

[21] Directive 97/66 has been replaced by Directive 02/58.

[22] The Data Retention amendment to Directive 02/58 by way of Directive 06/24 has been declared null by the European Court of Justice on April 2014 in the Judgment related to Joined Cases C-293/12

Nevertheless, from a legal taxonomy perspective, they provide a useful means by which to untangle the Gordian knot that ties privacy to data protection.

Apart from the semantic confusion generated by the cavalier use of the concept of 'privacy' in the titles of the data protection provisions, there is another fundamental difference between the two ideas. While the GDPR applies to natural persons only, the ePrivacy Directive (and its future upgrade, the ePrivacy Regulation) is meant to protect legal persons as well. And whereas the GDPR relies upon a complex notion of fairness in respect of the processing of personal data, the ePrivacy legislation is focused on protecting private life and confidentiality. Where the GDPR is enforceable against automatic and filing-system-oriented processing, the ePrivacy deals with a far wider spectrum of processing because its purpose is to protect legal rights rather than regulate the way data are processed.

This conclusion is supported by two key points of the ePrivacy Directive: recital numbers 4 and 7. The first states:

> (4) Directive 97/66/EC of the European Parliament and of the Council of 15 December 1997 concerning the processing of personal data and the protection of privacy in the telecommunications sector translated the principles set out in Directive 95/46/EC into specific rules for the telecommunications sector. Directive 97/66/EC has to be adapted to developments in the markets and technologies for electronic communications services in order to provide an equal level of protection of personal data and privacy for users of publicly available electronic communications services, regardless of the technologies used.

The second declares:

> (7) In the case of public communications networks, specific legal, regulatory and technical provisions should be made in order to protect fundamental rights and freedoms of natural persons and legitimate interests of legal persons, in particular with regard to the increasing capacity for automated storage and processing of data relating to subscribers and users.

This Directive – rightly – while establishing a common legal framework to protect both natural and legal persons, draws a distinction based upon the object of the protection: fundamental rights for human beings, on the one hand, and for non-human, legal fiction-created entities, legitimate interests (in terms of industrial secrecy, know-how protection and so on), as stated by recital 12, on the other.[23]

---

and C-594/12, *Digital Rights Ireland Ltd (C-293/12) v Minister for Communications, Marine and Natural Resources, Minister for Justice, Equality and Law Reform, Commissioner of the Garda Síochána, Ireland, The Attorney General, with the intervention of: Irish Human Rights Commission, and Kärntner Landesregierung (C-594/12), Michael Seitlinger, Christof Tschohl and others.*

[23] '(12) By supplementing Directive 95/46/EC, this Directive is aimed at protecting the fundamental rights of natural persons and particularly their right to privacy, as well as the legitimate interests of legal persons. This Directive does not entail an obligation for Member States to extend the application of Directive 95/46/EC to the protection of the legitimate interests of legal persons, which is ensured within the framework of the applicable Community and national legislation.'

Also relevant here are recitals 37 and 40. They first acknowledge that automatic call forwarding and unsolicited communications may cause distress to a natural person, and then affirm that a natural person should be given an appropriate safeguard against these intrusions. In so doing they sever the equivalence between 'privacy' protection and respect for private life. The nuisance created by an unsolicited call is clearly related to one's private life, but has little or no direct bearing on 'privacy'.

Article 5(3) of the Directive, also known as the 'cookie law', is a specific example of the inconsistency created by the semantic overlapping between privacy and data protection. The relevant paragraph reads:

> 3. Member States shall ensure that the use of electronic communications networks to store information or to gain access to information stored in the terminal equipment of a subscriber or user is only allowed on condition that the subscriber or user concerned is provided with clear and comprehensive information in accordance with Directive 95/46/EC, inter alia about the purposes of the processing, and is offered the right to refuse such processing by the data controller. This shall not prevent any technical storage or access for the sole purpose of carrying out or facilitating the transmission of a communication over an electronic communications network, or as strictly necessary in order to provide an information society service explicitly requested by the subscriber or user.

The rationale is commendable; it forbids stealth collection of users' information by way of hidden tracking technologies such as cookies, web beacons, and so on. Its enforcement, by contrast, has been proved legally unnecessary, technically confused, and practically useless.

In respect of the first of these three issues, it is worth pointing out that the general duty of information that rests on the data controller's shoulders under the Data Protection Directive, and, now, under the GDPR, is neither limited to nor hampered by a specific method of processing. In other words, what matters is the personal data collection, not the manner in which it is carried out. As soon as a data controller gathers personal data, whatever the tool (cookies included), it is under a duty to protect the information. There is therefore no need to restate the obvious or impose specific duties, which have been shown to actually weaken rather than reinforce users' rights, as demonstrated by the technical issues affecting the 'cookie law'.

Article 5(3) of the Directive addresses 'the use of electronic communications networks to store information or to gain access to information stored in the terminal equipment'. Technically speaking, this provision has a wide scope, from the remote software update/upgrade mechanism[24] to SSH session known hosts'

---

[24] The remote software update/upgrade mechanism works by collecting the version of the application and/or the operating system of a user, matching it with the software house versions, and sending the new piece of software straight to the user's computer.

local recording,[25] or TLS/SSL email, or the storage of website certificates.[26] Such activities may fall well within the scope of the data protection legislation as it is clear, at the same time, that nobody actually cared whether it did. This has simply been ignored, to be replaced by a web-based, 'One-Click-Privacy-Protection Check.'

Indeed, the experience of users' access to websites, especially when using small-screen devices such as smartphones, is bedevilled by pop-ups, banners and flickering windows offering links to a 'privacy policy' and a button to click to remove these irritations. All the user is required to do is close a window, click a checkbox or an 'OK' button and – and in theory at least – his or her 'privacy' is done![27]

In its Information Providers Guide, the European Commission states: 'The ePrivacy Directive – more specifically Article 5(3) – requires prior informed consent for storage or for access to information stored on a user's terminal equipment'. In other words, you must ask users if they agree to most cookies and similar technologies (eg web beacons, Flash cookies, etc) before the site starts to use them.

For consent to be valid, it must be informed, specific, freely given and must constitute a real indication of the individual's wishes. However, some cookies are exempt from this requirement. Consent is not required if the cookie is used for the sole purpose of carrying out the transmission of a communication, and strictly necessary in order for the provider of an information society service explicitly requested by the user, to provide that service.

Cookies clearly exempted from consent, according to the EU advisory body on data protection, Working Party 29 (WP29), include: user-input cookies (session ID) such as first-party cookies to keep track of the user's input when completing online forms, shopping carts, etc, for the duration of a session, or persistent cookies limited to a few hours in some cases, authentication cookies, to identify the user once he or she has logged in, for the duration of a session, user-centric security cookies, used to detect authentication abuses, for a limited persistent duration, multimedia content player cookies, used to store technical data to play back video or audio content, for the duration of a session, load-balancing cookies, for the duration of a session, user-interface customisation cookies such as language or font preferences, for the duration of a session (or slightly longer),

---

[25] SSH stands for Secure Shell and is the name of a cryptographic protocol to connect to a network resource through an insecure channel. When accessing a server for the first time, SSH warns the user that the remote IP address is not included in the local user's known hosts list and asks for the list to be updated.

[26] Secure Socket Layer (SSL) and Transport Layer Security (TLS) certificates are encrypted, digitally signed files to be stored into a server for secure identification purposes. By installing an SSL/TLS certificate into its servers, an organisation can provide users with evidence of its actual identity. Internet browsers such as Mozilla Firefox contain a list of valid certificates that can be updated by the user every time that a website he is trying to access asks him to install its own certificate (an act of faith that should be executed with the utmost care).

[27] These three flaws are well documented by the most authoritative enforcement agent of Article 5(3): Europa, the European Commission website itself.

and third-party social plug-in content-sharing cookies, for logged-in members of a social network.[28]

Ironically, Europa itself is not secure, in the sense that (at the time of writing) the site does not carry a SSL/TLS certificate to secure the communication exchange. Secondly, all the information provided to the users is 'cookie-centric' and 'cookie-centred'.

Thirdly, contrary to what both the Commission and the Article 29 Working Party (now mutated into the European Data Protection Supervisor) say,[29] not all tracking cookies require the data-subject's consent.

The syllogism is simple: consent is needed when processing personal data. A user accessing a website without logging-in or providing other proof of personal identification is anonymous, therefore no consent is required to invade the user's computer with whatever cookies, if the personal identity of the user is not collected.

This conclusion, as legally sound as it is, reveals a major problem in respect of the personal data legislation approach: the anonymity paradox. As mentioned, where there is no actual possibility for a data-controller to either identify or render identifiable a data-subject, data protection legislation does not come into play. But it does not follow that individual rights are secure or, more importantly, that personal information processing, since it is not connected to an identity, is harmless.

A data controller might not care about the name of the user who is behind the IP number 79.3.12.208 using a computer whose network name is *Administrators-Mac-Pro.local*. What matters is being able to build a profile about this faceless user, to send him or her 'relevant' information or, worse, to shape their thoughts by selecting, unbeknown to them, the content to display as output of their queries.

Hence, the paradox: privacy and personal space can be violated even if the data protection provisions are met, since there is no need to know somebody else's name in order to harass him or to invade his personal space when a computer and a network are involved. The same conceptual confusion affects the impending 'ePrivacy Regulation'[30] that will repeal Directive 2002/58/EC.

While the legislative process is still under way, the European Commission has already made clear its position on the matter. Both the communication to the EU Parliament that supports the proposal[31] and the legal text itself are still flawed by the semantic confusion already identified above in respect of the other EU legislation.

---

[28] European Commission, Information Providers Guide – http://ec.europa.eu/ipg/basics/legal/cookies/index_en.htm#section_2 (visited 2 June 2018.)

[29] Article 29 Data Protection Working Party Opinion 04/2012 on Cookie consent Exemption – http://ec.europa.eu/justice/data-protection/article-29/documentation/opinion-recommendation/files/2012/wp194_en.pdf.

[30] Regulation EU XXX/2019 concerning the respect for private life and the protection of personal data in electronic communications and repealing Directive 2002/58/EC.

[31] European Commission COM(2017) 10 final – Proposal for a Regulation of the European Parliament and of the Council concerning the respect for private life and the protection of personal data

Article 4(3)(c) defines electronic communications metadata as

> data processed in an electronic communications network for the purposes of transmitting, distributing or exchanging electronic communications content; including data used to trace and identify the source and destination of a communication, data on the location of the device generated in the context of providing electronic communications services, and the date, time, duration and the type of communication,

while Chapter II of the e-Privacy Regulation protects 'electronic communications of natural and legal persons and information stored in their terminal equipment', by imposing a mandatory consent requirement for the processing of metadata by way of a data-controller.

So, to summarise, legislation that is ostensibly designed to protect a human right (privacy), actually extends such protection from natural persons to legal persons. While the latter have the right to secrecy and confidentiality, they cannot be said to enjoy the right to privacy in the sense of control over (possibly) anonymous information (the metadata.)

Legal persons are no less entitled to some form of control over their information. Anonymous data processing may still infringe individual privacy even if handled in accordance to the data protection legislation.

While there is a need to address the protection of legal persons' information, it is unsatisfactory to equate natural and legal persons simply by declaring that the latter are entitled to privacy by virtue of the GDPR. Its purpose is to protect the personal data of natural persons when involved in automatic or filing-system-based processing.

An early Italian case involving the legal notion of personal data protection was heard by the First Branch of the Civil Court of Milan in 1999. It related to the claim of the second wife of a Mr Olcese who successfully requested the Italian Data Protection Authority to order a newspaper to cease attaching the family name to his first wife. In overruling the decision of the Data Protection Authority, the Milan court declared:

> In this regard, the Court must affirm ... that Law 675/96 – while in its introduction declares the 'purposes' of guaranteeing the 'respect of the rights, of the fundamental freedom, as well as the dignity' of the individual, 'with particular attention to confidentiality and personal identity' – ... can neither be considered like an actual 'general prerogative of an individual' nor dedicated more to protecting an individual person than regulating data processing. Such an interpretation is flawed by a defect of perspective, because it confuses different and non-fungible aspects like the law's rationale [protection of fundamental rights of the individual] and its operative perimeter [ie 'personal data processing']; only by a complementary integration of these different aspects is it

in electronic communications and repealing Directive 2002/58/EC (Regulation on Privacy and Electronic Communications), 10 January 2017: http://www.europarl.europa.eu/RegData/docs_autres_institutions/commission_europeenne/com/2017/0010/COM_COM(2017)0010_EN.pdf (visited 25 March 2018.)

possible to define thoroughly the legal object of the protection granted by the law: the fundamental rights of the individual with specific, and exclusive, reference to the implication of the personal data processing.[32]

An appeal against this decision was upheld by the Italian Supreme Court in 2001[33] on a minor question relating to the relationship between the EU and the Italian legal system, but the basis of its finding remains logically sound, as the Supreme Court did not strike it down.[34]

The distinction between data protection and privacy is acknowledged by the European Court of Justice. Its press release 84/2017 on the EU–Canada PNR transfer agreement includes an important (though unnoticed) statement:

> [T]he transfer of PNR [Passenger Name Records] data from the EU to Canada, and the rules laid down in the envisaged agreement on the retention of data, its use and its possible subsequent transfer to Canadian, European or foreign public authorities entail an interference with the fundamental right to respect for private life. Similarly, the envisaged agreement entails an interference with the fundamental right to the protection of personal data.[35]

This is not mere semantics. By reasserting the difference between privacy and data protection, the Court issued a (possibly unintended) warning to all of the parties (including data protection authorities) involved in the enforcement of data protection regulations. It states, in effect, that to interpret data protection laws as 'privacy laws' is mistaken, and weakens the protection of the personal information of individuals.

Despite the GDPR's attempt to provide fairly comprehensive protection to personal data, large holes remain in its fence.[36]

---

[32] English translation by Andrea Monti.

[33] *Corte di cassazione* First Civil Branch, Decision 30 June 1999 No 8889. The Court overruled the Milan decision, challenging the assumption of the lower court judge that the Italian Data Protection Law's reach was limited to automated and/or filing-system-oriented processing.

[34] Technically speaking, the Supreme Court was correct in overruling the decision of the Court of Milan. The then Italian Data Protection Act was not the formal means of enforcement of the Data Protection Directive. Thus, while being an almost verbatim transposition of the EU text, it was not bound by the limits set forth by the European legislation. Thus, the Italian Act extended the reach of the law from automated and/or filing-system-oriented processing to simply processing, no matter how it was carried out. Therefore, the Milan Court was wrong in enforcing the more limited definition set forth by the EU Data Protection Directive. But from an EU perspective, it was the Italian Parliament which was wrong when it passed a law that went well beyond the scope of the Directive on data protection. Thus, the basic tenet of the Court of Milan's decision about the legal significance of the right to protection of personal data is still valid, since it is now *jus receptum* all around the European Union that personal data protection is inextricably connected to automated and/or filing-system-oriented processing.

[35] European Court of Justice – Press Release no 84/2017 issued on 26 July 2017 – Opinion 1/15 – The Court declares that the agreement envisaged between the European Union and Canada on the transfer of PNR data may not be concluded in its current form: https://curia.europa.eu/jcms/jcms/p1_402881/en/ (visited 15 March 2018).

[36] In fact the GDPR gives rise to many problems in regard to its actual enforcement – from the competing role of the local data protection authorities, to the fragmentation, at the national level, of the legal provisions passed to harmonise the EU regulation with the single legal system. See, as an instance,

IV. The European Court of Human Rights

Contrary to the EU Charter of Fundamental Rights, the European Convention on Human Rights and Fundamental Freedoms relates only to the (Article 8) right to respect for private and family life, without any explicit reference to the protection of personal information. And, as already mentioned, the European Court of Human Rights has construed Article 8 extremely widely, well beyond any reasonable conception of either 'privacy' or 'personal information'. But, in view of the scope of the text of that article, it is not entirely surprising that this development has occurred. An inevitable consequence of so generous a construction is the relentless blurring of the distinction between data protection and the right to privacy as a subset of the right to respect of private and family life.

Several instances of this disturbing trend might be cited. A recent example is the Court's 2017 decision in *Fuchsmann v Germany*.[37] The plaintiff challenged the verdict of a German court that denied his request to have certain statements about him removed from the online edition of the *New York Times*. He called in aid the notorious European Court of Justice's *Google Spain* decision[38] about the existence of the 'right to be forgotten' (now included in Article 17 of the GDPR as a specific provision.)

This novel right was recognised by the European Court of Justice. It is supposed to enable users to delete their data where there are no legitimate grounds for retaining them. In a controversial, and potentially far-reaching, decision, it decided that the Directive supported the applicant's claim against Google to have an old newspaper report on his financial history deleted. The Court held that Google, despite being a search engine, was a 'controller' of the data it processes and provides. Data subjects were therefore able to request that search engines delete personal data from their search results, and, should they decline, to pursue legal action or complain to their data protection authority.

The effect of the judgment is to render search engine operators, as distinct from the original web page publishers, responsible for removing information on data subjects from search engine results even where the publication on the original pages might be lawful. And the Court added that the right to demand rectification, erasure, or blocking of data was not confined to instances where the

---

the public hearing held in the Italian Senate on 7 June 2018 where the Italian Association of Internet Providers raised a red flag on the impact of the announced local provisions over the way digital criminal investigations are carried out by prosecutors and law enforcement agencies: http://webtv.senato.it/webtv_comm_hq?video_evento=91 (the hearing starts at 4:00) (visited 10 June 2018.)

[37] European Court of Human Rights (Fifth Section), *Fuchsmann v Germany* Application no 71233/13, [2017] ECHR 925, judgment issued 19 October 2017, final 19 January 2018: https://hudoc.echr.coe.int/eng#{%22itemid%22:[%22001-177697%22]} See below.

[38] CJEU (Grand Chamber) Case C-131/12, *Google Spain SL, Google Inc v Agencia Española de Protección de Datos, Mario Costeja González*, 13 May 2014 (http://curia.europa.eu/juris/document/document_print.jsf?doclang=EN&docid=152065).

data was inaccurate, but extended to circumstances in which the processing was unlawful for any other reason, including non-compliance with any other ground in the Directive relating to data quality or criteria for data processing, or in the context of the right to object to data processing on 'compelling legitimate grounds'. It acknowledged that this right had to be balanced against other rights, especially freedom of expression, but the public interest in the information was relevant only where the data subject was a public figure.

The judges of the European Court of Justice recognised that the Directive's requirements that personal data must be retained for limited periods – only for as long as it is relevant – amounts to a form of the 'right to be forgotten'. A number of intriguing questions remain open. For example, when does personal data become irrelevant? Who is a public figure?

Within a few days of the ruling, hundreds of deletion requests were received by Google, including from an ex-politician seeking re-election, a convicted paedo-phile, and a medical doctor. In the following months, tens of thousands of requests were received. Almost a third related to fraud, one-fifth concerned serious crime, and 12 per cent were connected to child pornography arrests. Serious concern has been expressed that the ruling will result in censorship and will limit freedom of expression.

The European Court of Human Rights in *Fuchsmann* was unpersuaded by the plaintiff's objection. It denied the claim, resting its judgment on a balancing exer-cise between free speech and the protection of private life. It stated *obiter*:

> As far as the applicant complained that the article was also retrievable by merely search-ing online for his name, the Court notes that the applicant provided no information in his submissions regarding any efforts made to have the link to the article removed from online search engines.[39]

On the one hand, the Court accepts that the right to be forgotten has no relation-ship with Article 8 and must be enforced by way of a different legal framework; on the other, however, one could interpret its decision to mean that in order to invoke the right to be forgotten under Article 8, one must first seek to enforce it by way of the EU and domestic data protection legislation. But this would be a rather impractical and illogical outcome, and contrary to Article 17 of the GDPR. This is the case, first, because under this provision, of the six circumstances specified in paragraph (1) that can support a request to erase personal data, none is directly related to 'privacy'. Secondly, paragraph 3(a) clearly stipulates that the right to eras-ure is not enforceable in the case of processing that is necessary 'for exercising the right of freedom of expression and information.'

In fact, *Fuchsmann* supports the proposition that it is not possible to consider (the EU legal definition of) data protection as a synonym for either the right to respect of private life or its right of privacy component.

---

[39] *Fuchsmann v Germany*, n 37 above, [2017] ECHR 925, para 53.

V. Conclusion

This is not a retreat from the protection of fundamental rights. It is the reverse. But the combined effect of the expansive judicial interpretation of Article 8 – failing to acknowledge the difference between privacy and private life – and the elision of data protection and 'privacy' have generated an unacceptably elusive legal land-scape that undermines the safety of personal information.

The rhetoric of rights often generates complacency, especially when their enforcement relies on individual action. This is intensified when the claimed right bristles with ambiguity. Placing control of personal information at the heart of our deliberations about privacy achieves what the conventional Warren and Brandeis analysis has conspicuously failed to do.

3

Personal Information and Power

I. Introduction

From the dawn of history there has been a continual development of the idea that an individual has the right to control the lock that opens the door to his or her intimate self, and that privacy is not a static, mono-dimensional right.

> Privacy theory ... describes the individual's efforts to maintain voluntary control over the boundary between themselves and others in order to have freedom of engagement and disengagement and for behavior to be free of interference by others. A key element is the ability to avoid inappropriate or undesired disclosure. Privacy occurs along a continuum between the extremes of total social porosity and total isolation. The issue with privacy is not separation, per se, but control. The exercise of this control varies between people and also for any person across different situations.[1]

But to what extent is this 'control' untrammelled? And can the right to privacy stand its ground when confronted by collective interests, Realpolitik or simply raw power?

Historically surveillance, including mass surveillance, has always been a feature of power, and those who exert such power, irrespective of their particular ideology, have always relied upon the accumulation of information about their inhabitants, citizens or foreigners, to preserve their position:

> [I]ntelligence organizations are neither the product nor a feature of any one particular form of government. All governments need intelligence upon which to base their decisions, be their posture defensive or offensive, be they at war or at peace. Intelligence gathering is just as natural to democracies as it is to dictatorships. Although totalitarian regimes very often misuse their intelligence services, notably by taking advantage of domestic surveillance capabilities, nevertheless every government, authoritarian or representative, needs information about neighboring countries in order to consider its options and make educated decisions.[2]

---

[1] Michael R Eldstein, 'Privacy and Secrecy as Analytical Concepts' in Susan Maret (ed), *Government Secrecy* (*Research in Social Problems and Public Policy*, vol 19) (Bingley: Emerald Group Publishing, 2011) 24.

[2] Rose Mary Sheldon, *Intelligence Activities in Ancient Rome: Trust in the Gods but Verify* (*Studies in Intelligence*) (London: Routledge, Kindle edition, 2005) 36.

Nor would it be correct to think of *mass* surveillance as an activity that has been conceived and practised only in recent times. One can trace its origins to the Middle Ages, if not earlier.

While the Roman Republic, and, later, the Empire, did not engage in structured information-gathering, relying instead on a network of spies[3] and *agents provocateurs*[4] as a counter-insurgency tool, the Catholic Church has depended on the sacramental confession as an instrument of social control since the thirteenth century.[5] Indeed, this means of control continued to exert considerable influence over the Catholic Church's opposition to modernity, and it played a significant role in its support of the Inquisition. As Adriano Prosperi, member of the Lincean Academy and author of several essays on the Roman Inquisition in the sixteenth century, remarks:

> Insecurities and lacerations produced by the expansion of the then known world and by the beginning of the cultural unification process, made urgent the widespread use of control, by way of brutal repression when dealing with incoercible rebels, by continuous pressure on consciences when dealing with the rest of the population … On the Italian peninsula the Inquisition had a presence of a different kind. Here the building of a confessional homogeneity of the population was mainly obtained by emphasis placed upon the controlling of ideas through the censorship and above all by the very sweet, soothing and cunning channel of confession … [T]he proof of its effectiveness is shown by the depositions collected by the notaries of the Inquisition … Most of the complaints and denunciations, the original documents of which still exist, open by indicating that the defendant had been reported to the Inquisition tribunal by a confessor.[6]

The use of the sacramental confession and other measures provide a hint as to the potential of mass surveillance, its application and evolution in subsequent centuries. This includes thought-control by way of 'yin' expedients such as the forgiveness of a sinner's soul, and 'yang' methods such as the censorship of books, turning people into snitches, and infringements of the secrecy of private communications.

---

[3] 'To live in a city, where there are so many eyes to see and so many ears to hear things which are and are not, is a serious handicap for anyone who desires to play at revolution, unless he be wholly intent upon his own death. On the contrary, it prompts prudent and sensible people to walk slowly even when engaged in wholly permissible pursuits.' Philostratus, *Life of Apollonius* 8.7 quoted by Sheldon, *Intelligence Activities in Ancient Rome*, n 2 above, 162.

[4] 'In this fashion the rash are ensnared by the soldiers of Rome. A soldier, dressed like a civilian, sits down by your side, and begins to speak ill of Caesar, and then you too, just as though you had received from him some guarantee of good faith in the fact that he began the abuse, tell likewise everything you think, and the next thing is – you are led off to prison in chains.' Epictetus, *Discourses* 4.13.5, WA Oldfather (tr) (Loeb Classical Library edition, Cambridge MA, Harvard University Press) quoted by Sheldon, n 2 above, 288.

[5] *Omnis utriusque sexis*, the 21st Canon presented to the Fourth Lateran Council in 1215, dictated that every Christian of the proper age confess his or her sins at least once a year.

[6] Adrianio Prosperi, *L'Inquisizione romana: letture e ricerche* (Rome: Edizioni di Storia e Letteratura, 2003) xxvi–xxvii. Translated by Andrea Monti.

Oddly enough, the practice of structuring domestic intelligence was lost until the nineteenth century when the increasing need for internal security generated a renewed interest by rulers in the private lives of their citizenry:

> A more inward-looking intelligence specialism also developed, at varying rates over roughly the same period. This originated in the nineteenth-century 'secret policing' which appeared on the Continent in the first half of the century through the widespread fear of repetitions of the French Revolution. Police forces developed arrangements for surveillance, informers and mail interceptions. The earliest separate institution for this purpose was the Russian Third Section of the Imperial Chancery founded in 1826, which was later succeeded by the Okhrana and its eventual communist descendant, the KGB. After 1848 the fear of mass revolution declined, but communism and anarchism continued to present threats at a time when all policing was becoming more professional.[7]

It is at this very moment that technology meets politics, thanks to the emergence of the criminal investigation department, the application of scientific techniques to the problems of detection, apprehension, surveillance of, and storage of information about, crime and criminals.[8]

In the course of time, the practice of collecting and organising both public and private information about citizens was perfected, including the use of 'unharmful' census data. And without the support of information technology, since – despite the contemporary concern about Big Data accumulation – mass surveillance does not necessarily rely on powerful supercomputers, the Internet or artificial intelligence. An efficient and logically well-designed personal data management system, without (or with only limited) technical capabilities, has been shown to be extremely effective in achieving a comprehensive, large-scale 'management' of the citizens of a state, and others who represent a perceived threat to the state.

Of course, the needs of public policing can be satisfied by the intrusion into the private life of an individual. Nevertheless, this very goal requires the processing of publicly available and, prima facie innocuous, personal information.

The archetype of a politically oriented filing-system is the one established in Italy in 1894, when

> the circular n. 5116 of 25 May 1894 issued by the Directorate General of Public Security, established an office with the task of building and systematic updating the list of political opponents.
>
> Anarchists, republicans, socialists but also idlers and vagrants were the subject of a widespread surveillance activity that fed a substantial archive of personal files … During the Fascist period, the surveillance and control activity of the police was expanded up to

---

[7] Michael Herman, *Intelligence Power in Peace and War* (Cambridge: Cambridge University Press, 1996) 19.

[8] Christopher Dandeker, *Surveillance, Power, and Modernity: Bureaucracy and Discipline from 1700 to the Present Day* (New York: St Martin's Press, 1990).

include not only the politicians, but a whole indeterminate category of people, defined as generically anti-fascist, and the *Allogeni*, that is, the ethnic minorities mainly settled in the region of Venezia Giulia.[9]

These practices 'improved' over time and in the course of a few years mass surveillance became the standard method by which to protect 'national security'. Under Fascism, Mussolini expanded it to 'monitor' the highest members of the state and the Italian Royal Family,[10] and Germany's census modernisation prior to the Second World War, made possible by IBM's specially designed punch-card machines named 'IBM Hollerith', led directly to the Holocaust:[11]

> Once punched, the columns were imbued with personal information about the individual: county, community, gender, age, religion, mother tongue, number of children, current occupation, and second job, if any. 'Be Aware!' reminded huge block-lettered signs facing each cluster of data entry clerks. Instructions were made clear and simple. Column 22 Religion was to be punched at hole 1 for Protestant, hole 2 for Catholic, or hole 3 for Jew. Columns 23 and 24 Nationality were to be coded in row 10 for Polish speakers. After punching, the cards were shuttled to a separate section of the hall, where they passed through long, squat Hollerith counters at the rate of 24,000 per hour. The system kept track of its own progress. Hence, Dehomag was always aware whether it was on schedule. Once counted, the cards moved to the proofing section. No errors would be tolerated and speed was essential. Proofing machines tabulated and verified proper punching for more than 15,000 cards per hour. When Jews were discovered within the population, a special 'Jewish counting card' recorded the place of birth. These Jewish counting cards were processed separately.[12]

During this period, the United States used the Census Bureau to achieve a similar aim: interning American citizens of Japanese descent in concentration camps:

> Despite decades of denials, government records confirm that the U.S. Census Bureau provided the U.S. Secret Service with names and addresses of Japanese-Americans during World War II.
>
> The Census Bureau surveys the population every decade with detailed questionnaires but is barred by law from revealing data that could be linked to specific individuals. The Second War Powers Act of 1942 temporarily repealed that protection to assist in the roundup of Japanese-Americans for imprisonment in internment camps in California

[9] The *Casellario Politico Centrale* has been made available online by the Italian State Centralised Archive and can be accessed at: http://dati.acs.beniculturali.it/CPC/bancaDati.html.

[10] Aldo Giannuli, *Dossieraggio ad uso privato*, 20 August 2011: http://www.aldogiannuli.it/dossieraggio-ad-uso-privato/.

[11] On 16 June 1933, half a million census takers, recruited from the ranks of the 'nationalistically minded', went door-to-door gathering information. Cadres of Storm Troopers and SS officers were added to create a virtual census army. In some localities, when recruitment flagged, individuals were coerced into service. The interviews included pointed questions about the head of the household's religion and whether the person was in a mixed marriage: Edwin Black, *IBM and the Holocaust: The Strategic Alliance Between Nazi Germany and America's Most Powerful Corporation*, Expanded edn (Washington DC: Dialog Press, 2012) 56.

[12] Edwin Black, n 11 above, 58.

and six other states during the war. The Bureau previously has acknowledged that it provided neighborhood information on Japanese-Americans for that purpose, but it has maintained that it never provided 'microdata,' meaning names and specific information about them, to other agencies.

A new study of U.S. Department of Commerce documents now shows that the Census Bureau complied with an August 4, 1943, request by Treasury Secretary Henry Morgenthau for the names and locations of all people of Japanese ancestry in the Washington, D.C. area.[13]

A few decades later, during the Cold War, the Soviet Union and the other Iron Curtain countries adopted similar mass-control systems which entailed the violation of private lives. The former East Germany's *Staatssicherheitsdienst* (nicknamed 'Stasi') was notorious for its huge, paper-based filing system:

> The Ministry of State Security files, as everyone now knows, thanks to horrified media reports, took up several miles of space in the archives.
>
> While I do not contest that East German state security was afflicted by an obsessive desire to collect and file information on its citizens and those it perceived to be its enemies abroad, I would gently remind the headline writers that the reason for this was the primitive state of computerization in the East.[14]

Again, the Western bloc was not far behind the Warsaw Pact in the race for mass surveillance, as Markus Wolf wrote in his memoirs, 'I doubt the CIA is short of files, but I am sure it stores them more tidily on magnetic chips and tapes.'[15]

For decades the two sides of political surveillance, invading individuals' private lives, and collecting publicly available information on personal matters, have been, in theory, clearly separated. And this separation rendered it easier to distinguish between what is (or should be) privacy infringement and the dossier-building activity based on what today is grandly described as 'Open Source Intelligence'.

Western technological advances facilitated a major leap forward in the development of infrastructures devoted to the collection and analysis of huge amounts of information both for purposes of national security and policing, as the Echelon files,[16] such as Prism and its sibling, have dramatically demonstrated. But this 'progress' in surveillance technology would not have had reached its current pervasiveness without the self-induced self-disclosure that is now a ubiquitous feature of our social-networked world.[17]

---

[13] JR Minkel, *Confirmed: The U.S. Census Bureau Gave Up Names of Japanese-Americans in WW II* in *Scientific American*, 30 March 2007: https://www.scientificamerican.com/article/confirmed-the-us-census-b/.

[14] Markus Wolf, Anne McElvoy, *Memoirs of a Spymaster* (London: Pimlico, 1998) 330–31.

[15] ibid.

[16] Echelon, the global wiretapping network whose existence has been revealed by the investigative journalist, Duncan Campbell, in 'Somebody's Listening', *New Statesman*, 12 August 1988.

[17] Thanks, as will be demonstrated later, to the direct contribution of the individuals themselves, who seem unable to keep a single sneeze from their social networking profile!

Threats to the individual arise more from the 'creative' and subtle use of publicly available personal information, where there is not – and cannot be – a 'reasonable expectation of privacy', than from intrusions into home or office. In this context, it is now apparent that the (deliberate) mismanagement of publicly available personal information cannot be cured by the enforcement either of a right of privacy or of data protection laws. The question therefore arises whether there may be another right to be invoked in order to protect private life.

Matters are more complex when the needs of 'national security' are mingled with those related to investigations into criminal activity. In order to improve the efficacy of such investigations, the administration of criminal (and, to a lesser extent, civil) justice has also contributed to the creation of a new kind of citizens' database.

The precursor of the contemporary state-managed citizens' database for law enforcement purposes is the dataset collected in France around the end of the nineteenth century. This was based on the (questionable) scientific theories such as the *anthropometric* devised by Alphonse Bertillon,[18] the attempt to classify criminal archetypes by Cesare Lombroso,[19] and the more scientifically sound fingerprint processing devised at about the same time by the British scientist Sir Francis Galton.[20]

Traditional police databases and forensics filing systems are undoubtedly a source of concern for the protection of private life and for the right to privacy. They are, however, a minor annoyance compared with, a century later, the extensive range of instruments made available by science to the law enforcement community. National DNA database,[21] the Internet Traffic Data Retention,[22] and the accumulation of self-shared information in the golden cages of the social

---

[18] This forensic technique relied upon the then unverified assumption that some physical characteristics (arm length, head size and so on) were unique to a specific individual. Therefore, Bertillon thought, by collecting and storing such physical features it should be possible to build an archive and later compare the suspects with the recorded information, and identify both victims and perpetrators. In contrast to Sir Francisc Galton's still widely used fingerprint comparison technique though, Bertillonage was soon proven ineffective because of a fundamental scientific mistake (the parts of the body chosen as a standard reference were anything but invariant), and the lack of precise enough measurement tools that gave birth to an intolerable number of false positive results. But its legacy lives on in the various contemporary forensic databases that, more so than their predecessors, generate concerns not only in respect of the right to privacy. See Wilson Wall, *Genetics and DNA Technology: Legal Aspects*, 2nd edn (London: Routledge-Cavendish, 2004).

[19] Cesare Lombroso, *Studi per una geografia medica d'Italia* (Milan: G Chiusi, 1865).

[20] Francis Galton, *Finger Prints* (London and New York: Macmillan, 1892).

[21] Under Chapter 2, Article 2(1) of the Prüm Convention on the stepping up of cross-border cooperation, particularly in combating terrorism, cross-border crime and illegal migration, signed on 27 May 2005, '[T]he Contracting Parties hereby undertake to open and keep national DNA analysis files for the investigation of criminal offences. Processing of data kept in those files, under this Convention, shall be carried out subject to its other provisions, in compliance with the national law applicable to the processing.'

[22] Andrea Monti, 'The Legal Duty of IAPs to Preserve Traffic Data: A Dream or a Nightmare? (2004) 18(2) *International Review of Law Computers & Technology* 221.

networking platforms and contemporary communication devices are only some of the existing tools.

Oddly enough, these personal information collecting systems are poles apart in their relationship to a human being. The first deals with the nanocosm; the others are related to the sophisticated, psychological dimension of human behaviour. Both, however, achieve the same result: they create a single (or multiple) persona of an individual without actually knowing him or her, to be exploited for the social control techniques known as 'national security' and 'crime prevention' rather than for ex post facto investigatory purposes.

Historically, DNA-based investigation came first, thanks to the remarkable achievements of Sir Alec Jeffreys. Soon after having invented a method to connect DNA extracted from human tissue to its legitimate 'owner', the process assisted the British police in solving the so-called 'Black Pad murders'.[23] About 10 years later, Britain and the United States established the first DNA databases to support law enforcement investigations.[24]

II. Genetic Privacy

The results made possible by the analysis of a single bio-sample and the creation of forensics 'biobanks' raised several concerns about the possible misuse of these technologies in regard to the right of privacy, and to the notion of 'genetic privacy':

> Privacy experts generally distinguish four privacy concerns pertaining to DNA. First, there is physical privacy or *bodily privacy*. This comes into play at the point of DNA collection, whether it occurs for purposes of genetic testing, medical research, or criminal investigation ... Second, genetic privacy refers to *informational privacy*. Information contained within our genome is considered highly sensitive because it can reveal a vast amount of information about us ... This leads us to the third notion of privacy that is relevant to our DNA – familial or *relational privacy*. Because DNA is inherited, it can be examined to infer whether two individuals are related ... Finally, DNA can provide information about whether an individual was physically present at a certain location. A person's DNA found on a bedsheet at the scene of a crime is prima facie evidence that the person was at the location. In other words, DNA has implications for spatial or *locational privacy* (emphasis added).[25]

This again raises the question whether the issue at stake here is genuinely privacy. And does 'genetic privacy' actually exist?

---

[23] Michael Lynch, Simon A Cole, Ruth McNally and Kathleen Jordan, *Truth Machine: The Contentious History of DNA Fingerprinting* (Chicago IL: University of Chicago Press, 2010) 48–49.
[24] The UK National DNA Database was established in 1995, while the US Combined DNA Index System (CODIS) was created in 1998.
[25] Sheldon Krimsky, *Genetic Justice: DNA Data Banks, Criminal Investigations, and Civil Liberties* (Kindle Locations 4613–15). (New York: Columbia University Press, 2010).

While there is every reason to recognise the importance of bodily integrity as an element of personal control, autonomy, or self-determination over one's physical being, it is unhelpful to treat this as a feature of the right to privacy.[26] The notion of 'bodily privacy' is therefore best rejected.[27]

'Informational privacy' offers a more promising basis on which to rest the existence of so-called 'genetic privacy' since it speaks to the right of the individual to control the information that can be extracted from his or her genome and to prevent the sharing of sensitive medical information. But is such information any different from that contained in a patient's medical record? It reveals information about their current and previous conditions, about the probability of their succumbing to a specific illness, or their ability to recover from major surgery. This expansive concept of 'informational privacy' leads to a virtually infinite notion of 'privacy', as is explained in Chapter five.

Moreover, if the core of this supposed 'genetic-informational privacy' consists in the right to prevent others from deriving personal information from one's genome, would it not be more effective to consider 'privacy' in terms of personal information protection, regardless of its source?

In respect of the third element, 'relational privacy', one is bound to ask where the relationship with core privacy interests is. Deciding not to be informed about the prospects of suffering from a disease bears no relationship to the infringement of an individual's personal information.

The idea of 'locational (or 'spatial' privacy') is no less problematic.[28] There is, as a general rule, no legitimate or reasonable expectation of privacy in a public place. The fact that you happen to see me in the High Street at noon and you retain this information cannot sensibly be regarded as personal information – unless, of course, it is related to some other information about me that could be described as personal. So, for example, my being observed in a hospital carrying a suitcase might suggest that I am about to be admitted for treatment. Similarly, being seen in the company of another individual could suggest something other than an innocuous meeting.

In the light of the advances in geo-localisation technology, this conclusion may seem counterintuitive. Yet a violation of privacy requires more than raw

---

[26] Among her list of 10 'central human capabilities' Martha Nussbaum includes 'bodily integrity' which she defines as '*the ability* to move freely from place to place; to be secure against violent assault, including sexual assault and domestic violence; having opportunities for sexual satisfaction and for choice in matters of reproduction'. See Martha Nussbaum, *Frontiers of Justice: Disability, Nationality, Species Membership* (Boston MA: Harvard University Press, 2006) 76–78, discussed in Raymond Wacks, *Justice: A Beginner's Guide* (London: Oneworld, 2017) chapter 7.

[27] The House of Lords in *Wainwright v Home Office* [2003] UKHL 53 was unwilling to treat a strip search as a violation of Article 8. It rejected a complaint by Mrs Wainwright and her son who, when visiting another son in prison, were strip-searched in breach of prison rules and suffered humiliation and distress. The invasive search could not give rise to a claim in damages unless it was a tort or a breach of statutory duty. The court held that, although 'privacy' was an important value, the law did not recognise a right to privacy.

[28] Cf Graeme Laurie, *Genetic Privacy: A Challenge to Medico-Legal Norms* (Cambridge: Cambridge University Press, 2002).

geographical information about a person's whereabouts. What renders my itinerary or static location worthy of protection, or interesting to others, is the *reason* why an individual is somewhere, and not the mere fact of their physical presence in a specific place.

The similarity of this approach to data protection might lead one to conclude that, whether this right is called 'privacy' or not, it is covered by European Union legislation. But this is not the case. As argued in Chapter two, data protection legislation applies only when the data in question are either part of a filing system or automatically processed. The right to privacy – and specifically the protection of personal information – pertains to non-public personal information, even when processed outside the boundaries of the EU data protection regulations.

III. National DNA Databases

Nor is privacy, properly so called, involved when, say, the presence of a bio-sample at a crime scene facilitates the identification by the police of a suspect. First, from the perspective of a criminal trial, the mere presence of a hair or other bio-sample is insufficient proof that its 'owner' was indeed present at the scene of the crime. There may well have been 'secondary transfer' of this evidence. Unless specific conditions, such as the source of the DNA being human tissue such as blood or seminal fluids, all that can be derived from a piece of DNA is that sometime, somewhere, somebody (not necessarily its 'owner') placed the bio-sample there. In other words, the question of privacy simply does not arise.

Secondly, on a practical level, the very purpose of criminal investigation is to establish who was where and with whom. The police cannot legitimately be deprived of this evidence.

Thirdly, even if the bio-sample was found in a *private* place where those involved were engaged in non-public activities (a privacy-protected space, in other words), it would be preposterous to prohibit a police investigation from obtaining such evidence on the strength of an abstruse notion of 'privacy'.

It is, of course, true that being entered 'into the system' in this way constitutes an enforced disclosure of sensitive information about one's genetic heritage. A person has become an unintended subject of a criminal investigation, and must live with the stigma of being labelled a suspect or worse. But these factors have less to do with the disclosure or use of personal information than a general respect for private life (in its widest sense), human dignity, and physical integrity. This conclusion is equally true for both the taking of a single DNA sample and the creation of the UK's NDNAD (national DNA database.)

The latter has been condemned as a violation of privacy; this charge relates to the method of collecting bio-samples, as well as to the performing of familial searches in order to determine whether the genetic code of an unknown suspect resembles that of another (innocent) individual. Yet without access to this evidence, criminal investigations would be severely hampered.

Much of the criticism directed at forensic genetic databases is superficial and misinformed. Such databases actually consist of two separate entities: a biobank that contains tissues and other bio-samples, and a computerised database that stores the genetic profiles extracted from the bio-samples. The forensic evidence requirements, ie seeking a match between a profile extracted by a sample retrieved at the crime scene and sample(s) taken from the suspect(s) can be satisfied by merely retaining the profile, and discarding the tissue once the genetic sequence has been extracted. This solution is, however, disapproved of by the law enforcement community whose general position is that samples should be retained 'just in case':

> Retaining DNA samples from individuals is not necessary in order to avoid miscarriages of justice, because a second DNA sample is always taken from someone being prosecuted, to confirm the match with the DNA profile from the crime scene. This second match, rather than that in the NDNAD, is used in court proceedings. The stored DNA samples are also not used in criminal investigations because it is the DNA profile from the NDNAD that is used for comparison with the DNA profile from the crime scene.
>
> The NDNAD Board argues that samples must be kept for quality control and to check for errors. However, samples need not be kept permanently; they could be stored for a limited time until an investigation is complete. The Board also argues that keeping samples allows the NDNAD to be upgraded in order to use more detailed profiles in the future. Although this was necessary when the NDNAD was first created, it is likely to be costly and impracticable given its current size, and would make the NDNAD incompatible with other databases internationally. It is also always possible to obtain a more detailed profile from the second DNA sample that is taken from the defendant for use in court.[29]

What matters in regard to respect for private life in this context is the possibility of using the bio-samples to carry on further analysis unrelated to its original, strictly limited investigative purpose.

As the GeneWatch report said as far back as 2006 in relation to the UK's NDNAD:

> The data stored in the NDNAD in combination with access to the stored samples could offer a wealth of information for researchers interested in studying criminal behaviour. There have already been studies that have tried to find genes linked to [a propensity to commit] violent or sexual crimes or to find ways to use genetic tests to predict which people are more likely to re-offend.[30]

This shift from the original purpose that justifies the establishment of the NDNAD to other matters unrelated to criminal investigations is a major issue in regard

---

[29] Helen Wallace, *The UK National DNA Database: Balancing Crime Detection, Human Rights and Privacy* EMBO Rep. 7 July 2006, special number, S26–S30 – doi: 10.1038/sj.embor.7400727.

[30] K Staley, *The Police National DNA Database: Balancing Crime Detection, Human Rights and Privacy* (GeneWatch UK, January 2005) 37. http://www.genewatch.org/uploads/f03c6d66a9b354535738483c-1c3d49e4/NationalDNADatabase.pdf.

to privacy, or, more specifically, to the need to limit privacy protection for 'the greater good'.

A genetic sequencing database is sufficient to fulfil the investigative requirements of the police for both hot and cold cases, and is a legitimate component of the administration of justice. But allowing the state to retain the bio-samples and use them to determine future criminal behaviour or, worse, personal behaviour or attitudes, blurs the line between the administration of justice, on the one hand, and social control (including a form of genetic racism), on the other.

Strictly speaking, attitudes and future behaviour prediction are unrelated to privacy. Genetic analysis in these fields has not yet provided reliable scientific results. Nevertheless, from a legal perspective, even if it becomes possible to predict future attitudes or behaviour, this incubus would be one of social control rather than privacy.

The quest for a genetic root of social deviance leads to the return to the Third Reich's criminal law approach based on the *Täterschuld* (the idea that merely belonging to a group or to a category deserves punishment) or on the *Gesinnungsstrafrecht* (punishment is deserved simply because an individual chose to be what he is, regardless of whether he commits an offence).This risk is real, since the data of only a small section of the population is designed to be held by the NDNAD. Chapter five further analyses this issue, with the addition of the results of neuroscience.

Ideally, the most efficient national DNA database would contain the genetic profiles of the entire population. This 'democratic' solution would facilitate maximum identification of suspects of crime, and, probably, an increase in the number of indictments. But, apart from the technical difficulties, this would be an extreme position that few, if any, democratic societies would be willing to adopt.

While some countries, such as Italy, restrict the inclusion in the national DNA database to persons actually convicted of specific crimes (oddly, white-collar crime is excluded) or serving custodial sentences. Other jurisdictions, such as the United Kingdom, have extended the scope to incorporate those who have been cautioned or detained.

This is not the place to analyse the political implications of targeting specific crimes as a genetic profiling source. Suffice it to say that if, for instance, only the authors of violent crimes are to be included in the national DNA database, and such violent crimes are mainly committed by members of a certain race or social class, the statistics based on the database-supported convictions will inevitably yield information that, notwithstanding its limited value, is likely to influence lawmakers toward targeting that specific group.

IV. Where is 'Privacy'?

Even a broad concept of privacy, along the lines of Warren and Brandeis' right to be let alone, does not afford a legal basis upon which to preclude the use of bio-samples stored in a national DNA database for further research activities. Nor is the concept of privacy as the control of personal information, as proposed in this book, appropriate here, for the central question in this context is the extent to which the prevention of crime is to be weighed against not privacy, but the individual's cluster of rights to protection against unreasonable search and seizure, due process, probable cause, and a fair trial.

It is hardly surprising that not being content with the widespread use of genetic profiling, the attention of the state has extended to the enormous quantity of information related to individuals generated by personal computers and smartphones, and collected and stored by telecommunication companies, Internet Service Providers (ISP) and Over-the-Top (OTT) platforms.[31]

As in many other cases, when discussing technology, power and social control, the idea of deriving information about people by analysing the 'electronic breadcrumbs' they let fall while communicating is anything but new. During both World Wars the exploitation of the radio waves as a military communication tool led to the development of the so-called 'Signal Intelligence' (SigInt)[32] as an aspect of military intelligence-gathering based on the interception and decoding of an enemy's wireless transmissions to deduce information about a foe from the source, destination, time, and duration of a radio signal.[33]

Telephone records analysis has also long played an important part both in the intelligence and criminal investigation fields. Finally, with the arrival of the Internet and the frenzy of social networking and smartphone mania, we have ourselves constructed the most pervasive and impressive global surveillance and mass control system, which no single government even dared to dream of, by freely revealing not only traditional, SigInt information (places, dates, times, personal connections), but even intimate details about ourselves and others.

The amount of raw information currently available by way of Internet platforms and services is exceeded only by the information that can be derived by the interconnection of these raw digital breadcrumbs. And as if this were not enough, the wall that separates intelligence/law enforcement databases from others is crumbling slowly but surely.[34]

This brief account of the evolution of the surveillance and social control strategies is far from exhaustive, but underscores the thesis of this book that at the heart of the protection of privacy is the control of personal information.

---

[31] See Heinrich Drost, *Das Ermessen des Strafrichters* (Cologne: Heymann, 1930) 206.

[32] John Ferris, *The British Army and Signals Intelligence During the First World War* (London: Alan Sutton, 1992).

[33] Peter Matthews, *SIGINT: The Secret History of Signals Intelligence in the World Wars* (Kindle Locations 169–70) (The History Press. Kindle edition, 2013).

[34] Law enforcement investigators have been able to run a genetic familial search simply by sending a DNA sample collected at a crime scene to a facility that offers ancestry genetic searches, without the need for a court order. See Justin Poulsen, 'Your relative's DNA could turn you into a suspect', Wired.com (October 2015): https://www.wired.com/2015/10/familial-dna-evidence-turns-innocent-people-into-crime-suspects/ (visited 18 July 2018.)

Technically speaking, every time we use a computer, either stand-alone or connected to a network, a certain number of 'digital breadcrumbs' are created by the operating system and/or the higher-level software applications about what actions are executed locally and remotely. These events are recorded in a logfile whose main use is to perform troubleshooting activities and, in the case of a network connection, to allow the retrieval of the data asked by the remote server.

Deciding to enable and maintain these logfiles has long been the decision of the IT manager, but as sales activities moved online and new, specific services based on data-gathering were offered in certain business contexts such as retail services of various kinds, the fate of the logfiles fell to the company's marketing managers. It took less than a decade for the law enforcement community, and thus, for the politicians, to understand the usefulness of the logfiles and their retention for investigative purposes.

Hence, in the summer of 2002 the EU adopted Directive 2002/58, whose article 15(1) reads: 'Member States may, inter alia, adopt legislative measures providing for the retention of data for a limited period justified on the grounds laid down in this paragraph.' And later in the same year the EU Justice and Home Affairs Council adopted an official position, affirming that:

> [B]ecause of the significant growth in the possibilities afforded by electronic communications, data relating to the use of electronic communications is now a particularly important and useful tool in the investigation and prosecution of crime, in particular organised crime.[35]

Two years later, in 2004, the European Council took a further step along the road towards mandatary data retention. In its declaration of 25 March 2004 it officially endorsed this solution, setting up the agenda for its deployment: 'Priority should be given to the proposals under the retention of communication traffic data … with a view to adoption by June 2005.'[36]

Finally, in 2006 the EU passed Directive 2006/24/EC that made traffic data retention mandatory within the whole of the Union:[37] '[T]his Directive shall apply to traffic and location data on both legal entities and natural persons and to the related data necessary to identify the subscriber or registered user.' The fact that later, in 2014, the European Court of Justice (CJEU) demolished the directive does not affect the issues raised by the retention of traffic data, because the Court ruled

---

[35] Press Release C/02/404 – 2477th Council meeting – Justice and Home Affairs – Brussels, 19 December 2002: http://europa.eu/rapid/press-release_PRES-02-404_en.htm?locale=en (visited 30 July 2018.)

[36] European Council, *Declaration on Combating Terrorism*, Brussels 25 March 2004: http://www.consilium.europa.eu/uedocs/cms_data/docs/pressdata/en/ec/79637.pdf (visited 30 July 2018.)

[37] Directive 2006/24/EC of the European Parliament and the Council on the retention of data generated or processed in connection with the provision of publicly available electronic communications services or of public communications networks and amending Directive 2002/58/EC: https://eur-lex.europa.eu/LexUriServ/LexUriServ.do?uri=OJ:L:2006:105:0054:0063:EN:PDF (visited 30 July 2018.)

only on the extension and not the lawfulness of the legislation.[38] It held that a proportionate preservation of traffic data and location is an acceptable limitation to the protection accorded to private life and personal data. But while it is clear that private life and personal data might be negatively affected by 'carpet' traffic data retention, it is, yet again, difficult to discern how the right to privacy is undermined.

This CJEU landmark decision on data retention unequivocally supports the assumption that when national security, crime prevention, and the administration of justice are concerned, privacy is generally outweighed. But the Court fails to take into account that while in theory public security, crime prevention, and the administration of justice are supported by a very different rationale that makes it easy to determine whether the state has exceeded its democratic limits, this is no less true in reality.

The continuous shift from the administration of justice toward the prevention of crime and 'fighting terrorism' – together with the powerful push of the European Commission toward creating a duty (and, hence, the power) on the part of Internet Service Providers to remove 'illegal' content and interfere directly with users' online activity – creates a very uncertain scenario in which it is unclear where the right to privacy is supposed to stand.

Of course, the processing of traffic data can reveal information of an intimate nature, but not necessarily. In any event, most non-public online activity is protected by the right to secrecy of communication. So, even though an ISP has the technical means to access such data and use it for further processing, it is not permitted to do so.

Secondly, unless there is some sort of connection between the subject who has the credentials to access a service, and the individual who is at that moment using those credentials, there is no simple way to associate the traffic data with an identified person. This is what happens, for instance, when browsing a website belonging to a third party: unless the user discloses his or identity, anonymity is assured.

Thirdly, secrecy protection tools are widely available and perfectly legal. Therefore a user can access a network and engage in intimate or non-public activities such as accessing medical data or participating in political discussion groups.

It is important to understand – as this case clearly demonstrates – that the right to confidentiality or secrecy of communication is more powerful than the right of privacy in respect of the protection of the individual.[39] The individual is

---

[38] In its press release, the Court stated demolish that 'by adopting the Data Retention Directive, the EU legislature has exceeded the limits imposed by compliance with the principle of proportionality.' https://curia.europa.eu/jcms/upload/docs/application/pdf/2014-04/cp140054en.pdf (visited 30 July 2018).

[39] The English law of confidence, unlike that of several European jurisdictions, requires that in order to be protected the information must, inter alia, have the necessary 'quality of confidence', see Raymond Wacks, *Privacy and Media Freedom* (Oxford: Oxford University Press, 2013) 129 ff.

not without protection, albeit not in the name of 'privacy' as understood in these pages. When a court authorises a body-search or seizure of geolocation data, or the analysis of traffic data to establish a connection between individuals, it is misguided and superfluous to invoke a putative right to privacy. The bastions of a democratic society provide adequate protection in the shape of due process and the right to a fair trial. The appeal to 'privacy', for the reasons set out in Chapter one invites incoherence, uncertainty, and weakens the very right that it is sought to protect.

One question remains to be addressed: does the right to privacy play a role at least in crime prevention and national security? These activities are not, strictly speaking, subjected to prior judicial control as a means of protecting individual rights.

The answer to this question lies beyond the law. The paradigm shift in the exercise of state power has made global surveillance, mass accumulation of data, and the infringement of the secrecy of communication not only a technical reality, but a socially accepted condition. There is a clash between citizens' rights and the will of the state to know as much as possible about its people in accordance with the Nazi slogan 'nothing to hide, nothing to fear'.

This use of 'fear' has generated a blind acceptance of global remote and preemptive control. From mandatory data retention to state-manned malware, the promise of crime prevention has become a companion of the national security justification for violating individual rights. In this context data retention (combined with the arbitrary, and often clumsy, criteria of data analysis and clustering) plays a key role, because it encourages the creation of as many 'behaviour patterns' as suit the whims of whoever is searching, or whoever has access to the data.

We know, from practical experience, that commercial 'profiling' is ineffective; but even when it does work, it is much less effective than other, less intrusive ways of developing customer relations. Nevertheless the use of profiling has caused not only justified concern, but also exaggerated alarm. As a result, while there are attempts to limit profiling as a commercial tool, it is (quite wrongly) assumed that it can work wonders in criminal investigations, or for other controls of human attitudes and behaviour that are much less legitimate or justifiable. With the use of tools that are often unreliable, and can be easily manipulated, inquiries and trials are deployed against 'virtual identities' that can be created ad hoc on the basis of prejudice or a variety of questionable intentions. The myth of 'machine infallibility' combines with the obnoxious notion of 'criminal personality'. The key point is that vigilance is required in order to defend individual rights and personal freedom, not merely in respect of privacy.[40] Orwell, as always, was prophetic:

> As short a time ago as February, the Ministry of Plenty had issued a promise (a 'categorical pledge' were the official words) that there would be no reduction of the chocolate

---

[40] Giancarlo Livraghi, 'Civil rights and ambiguity of crime 'prevention', 24 January 2004: http://gandalf.it/free/datret.htm (visited 30 July 2018.)

ration during 1984. Actually, as Winston was aware, the chocolate ration was to be reduced from thirty grammes to twenty at the end of the present week. All that was needed was to substitute for the original promise a warning that it would probably be necessary to reduce the ration at some time in April.[41]

Certain that no-one recalled Big Brother's incorrect prediction about chocolate rations, Winston Smith was able to ensure that nobody could prove the Party wrong. This is a piquant illustration of the manner in which the control of personal information extends far beyond 'mere' privacy infringement and becomes a fundamental element in manufacturing consent for political ends, but also for less ambitious goals: selling goods and services, the subject of the next chapter.

[41] George Orwell, *Nineteen Eighty-Four* (Boston MA: Houghton Mifflin Harcourt, 1983) 38.

4

Personal Information, Goods and Services

> You load sixteen tons and what do you get?
> Another day older and deeper in debt.
> Saint Peter don't you call me 'cause I can't go.
> I owe my soul to the company store.
>
> *Merle Travis*

I. Introduction

Little has changed in the 72 years since Merle Travis penned his musical indictment of materialism. Mining companies often lured miners into purchasing goods that they were unable to afford. This led to their incurring onerous debts. A similar cavalier attitude characterises so-called 'web companies' such as Facebook, Google, and Amazon that have not only seized a large share of the market to create a quasi-monopoly, but, like the robber barons of old, have managed to influence politicians and policy-makers, and reshape the contours of fundamental rights, including free speech and privacy, to enhance their profit.

The debate over 'robber barons' began in the United States some 10 years before Travis's legendary song. In 1934 Matthew Josephson described

> a small class of men who arose at the time of our Civil War and suddenly swept into power. The members of this new ruling class were generally, and quite aptly, called 'barons,' ... They were aggressive men, as were the first feudal barons; sometimes they were lawless; in important crises, nearly all of them tended to act without those established moral principles which fixed more or less the conduct of the common people of the community ... These men were robber barons as were their medieval counterparts, the dominating figures of an aggressive economic age.[1]

They played a leading role in turning the United States of America from an agricultural-based society into an industrial power. In their relentless[2] pursuit of private

---

[1] Matthew Josephson, *The Robber Barons* (New York: Harcourt, Brace and Co, 1934) foreword.

[2] 'Relentless' was the original name the founder of Amazon, Jeff Bezos (now the wealthiest person in the world) chose for his corporation.

gain, the robber barons seized the country's natural resources and established control over its core infrastructures: energy, transport, communications, becoming more powerful than politicians.

II. Digital Robber Barons

Substitute 'railway' with 'network'; 'car' with 'computer' and 'oil' with 'information' and the current scenario differs only slightly. It is no exaggeration to claim that we now face a new generation of robber barons in the form of IT manufacturers, software, search engines and Internet platform companies that build their wealth by luring users into parting with their personal information gratis.

By exploiting the idea that personal information is provided free, the 'giants of the Web' are shaping our public and private habits and altering the relationship between citizen and power, with the overriding object of profit maximisation. Echoes of the era of the Vanderbilts and Rockefeller resound.

The first association made between the concept of robber barons and the IT world dates back to mid-2000. Accused of having purchased for its offices tens of thousands of Microsoft Windows pre-installed personal computers (while the USA were pressing charges against Microsoft in respect of its monopoly in the IT market), the then US Attorney General, Janet Reno, declared: 'America was not made the industrial giant of the world by the robber barons alone'.[3] She then pointed out that the Justice Department was trying to create competition so that there will be alternatives to 'robber barons', even though it still buys computers installed with Microsoft Windows.[4] In the words of Giancarlo Livraghi,

> Today's robber barons argue that because it's a 'new economy' the concepts of the past don't apply. It may be true that some new elements need to be considered … But the railways and the telegraph were as revolutionary in the nineteenth century as information technology and the internet are today. Many of the stock swindles of the past crossed borders … Everyone agrees that information is the driving force in the economy and society. That means that no one can be allowed to own it or control it.[5]

Modern robber barons found their way in the IT world as soon as computers and software became products that could be sold in huge quantities, thus becoming ubiquitous. They extended their reach as soon as the Internet turned from a geek-only club into a 'free-for-all' playground.

Since the late 1980s, the idea of setting (personal) information free was the mantra of the Cyberpunk and other libertarian movements. Around a decade later

---

[3] 'Reno defends MS purchases', *Wired*, 1 June 2000: https://www.wired.com/2000/06/reno-defends-ms-purchases/.
[4] ibid.
[5] Giancarlo Livraghi '"Robber Barons" Aren't New', issue 51 *NetMarketing*, 18 October 2000: http://gandalf.it/netmark/netmar51.htm (visited 10 August 2018).

the control of (personal) information became the key component of the digital robber barons' business. Oddly enough, though, the principal reason that has led the IT giants to pry into individuals' private lives has been the mundane need to protect intellectual property rather than the enforcement of an Orwellian, sales-oriented 'profiling' or 'behaviour-tracking' system.

In the beginning of the software-for-the-masses industry, between the late 1980s and the early 1990s, emerging power-mongers such as Microsoft evinced little concern about the unauthorised duplication of their computer programs. It was a simple matter to make copies of MS-DOS, as well as of Windows (until version 3.1), for there were no effective copy-protection measures in place. And this was not because of a lack of technical options.

In the then contemporary micro-computer field, when the rivalry between the British ZX Spectrum and the American Commodore 64 garnered large headlines, video games were heavily shielded thanks to rather sophisticated techniques. Copy removal programs such as the famous Lerm Tape Copier 7 were ubiquitous in the toolbox of just about every Sinclair user, as tape-to-tape loaders were the nightmare of Commodore 64 games manufacturers. In short, as counterintuitive as it may sound, in 1984 it was considerably more difficult to produce a copy of *Jet Set Willy*, a ZX Spectrum videogame, than one of Microsoft's MS-DOS v. 3.

Was this a deliberate choice of the 'serious' software industry? There are studies that hint at this hypothesis,[6] but there is no positive evidence to support this conclusion. In fact, when the Internet reached offices and homes, the onerous and frustrating copy protection systems suddenly became user-friendly and – this is important – transparent.

Between 1998 and 2003 Microsoft progressively enforced its product activation system on a wider scale, by forcing the user either to connect remotely to the software house facilities via the Internet, or call a number to obtain an unlock code. As in an *excusatio non petita*, the instructions that came together with the product activation process candidly informed users that Microsoft was committed to users' privacy. In particular, Microsoft claimed that it did not collect personal information, limiting its data gathering to the computer's technical features in order to establish whether its software had been (re)installed on the same computer or within the permitted number of devices.

But what prevented Microsoft, and other software houses, large and small, from breaking this promise? Nothing but their own undertakings. Once a remote

---

[6] 'Any software firm would like to see the market adopt its product. However … new software may be unattractive to customers until a large number of other customers have … established a user base … As a consequence, the customers may all remain lodged in the initial state of nonadoption, and the product will fail. In such a situation, it may be possible to first shift some individuals from nonadoption to piracy and to use piracy strategically to establish the initial network.' Ernan Haruvy, Vijay Mahajan, Ashutosh Prasad, 'The Effect of Piracy on the Market Penetration of Subscription Software' (2004) 77(2) *Journal of Business* 81–107 http://www.utdallas.edu/~eharuvy/papers/Piracy.pdf (visited 10 August 2018).

controller can access a computer, the only guarantee that it does not snoop around the intricacies of a user's hard disk is the controller's word. The reality, however, is that there is no genuine, reasonable expectation of privacy when somebody is allowed to access, unannounced, your computer. In other words, the 'urge' to fight 'software piracy' to 'protect innovation and investments' established a technical infrastructure of global control that later, after the user grew accustomed to the idea, was transformed into a real privacy threat thanks to the subterfuge of 'freebies' and 'personal recommendations'.

But the digital robber barons' club was not intended to include only software houses and IT manufacturers among its members. For in the early' 90s an assortment of new members joined the club: Amazon, eBay, Google, and about a decade later, Facebook, and the other major players in the social networking/entertainment business.

The common factor shared by IT companies, e-commerce and auction platforms, video games, online playing systems, nappy manufacturers and everything else that is connected to, or sold through, the Internet is the 'user registration' procedure. Nowadays nobody actually challenges this requirement; it seems self-evident that in order to buy something on Amazon or to sell your ceramic dog statue on eBay you need an 'account'. While this is not entirely true in the case of e-commerce activities, it is completely false in relation to software, services, and hardware of various kinds.

There are no technical or legal hurdles that prevent the purchase process from being reduced to minimal personal data in order to transact a sale or purchase. At most, it might be useful to retain a name, address, and possibly a VAT ID for the official record, and leave the payment to the e-payment provider (who, equally, does not need to know the object of the purchase). The same scenario works for auction-based services: a platform simply handles the technicalities of the transactions, but does not maintain additional information. When I subscribe to a 'free' club of users of my favourite toothpaste, why should I provide information about myself rather than just an alias or nickname? Similarly, when you buy a computer, a tablet, or a smartphone, let alone software, why should 'registering' be a condition of using the device/application for which you just paid?

Although stated with several nuances, the common answer to this question is 'because it benefits the user.' By registering, and thus (unnecessarily) revealing his or her identity, along with other information, the user obtains a number of 'goodies' in exchange, such as a history of purchases, counterpart identity verification, fraud protection, discount coupons, data backup and so on. All for free.

This answer would be correct, save for one small matter. While it is true that the user benefits from access to these additional services and information, why should the seller/provider/platform handler/hardware manufacturer be entitled to the same access? The provider will, naturally, contend that by accessing these data it is possible to better engineer the internal processes in regard to logistics, resource assignment and so on. To this response, privacy campaigners understandably reply that these avaricious companies have turned us into fish swimming in a transparent bowl, thereby compelling us to inhabit a *Truman Show* world by manufacturing our needs and controlling our will.

Both of these perspectives might, to some extent, be true in respect of goals, and this perception is reinforced by the brilliant achievements of companies such as Amazon, and by the scandals that occasionally surface in the mainstream media such as those involving Facebook/Cambridge Analytica or the alleged Russian attempt to influence the US presidential election.

III. Online Profiling

Many privacy campaigners adopt an instrumental notion of privacy that reduces the value of this fundamental right: if privacy merits protection merely because profiling allows the digital robber barons to shape our thinking, then protecting privacy as such is worthless. Privacy ought to be an end in itself. That a digital robber baron amasses a vast amount of personal information about an individual, before determining what he proposes to do with it, does, of course raise privacy concerns. But it is a mistake to generalise an issue that has an extensive, but still limited, reach in terms of privacy. The reality is that traditional 'profiling' or, as it is often called, 'market segmentation' employs different approaches based either on physical or psychological information:

> One class of segmentation approaches utilises the physical attributes of consumer populations that have not been established exclusively for marketing purposes, but nonetheless have proved to have relevance for defining market segments in consumer contexts. Another class of approaches is more closely tied to marketing objectives and depends upon the measurement of consumer behaviours and the psychological variables that underpin those behaviours.[7]

Online profiling collects various kinds (and extraordinarily large amounts) of information, ranging from the purely physical (geo-location, ethnicity, gender, age, employment, social status, wages etc) to more private (behavioural patterns in the use of services or purchase habits) and personal (psychographic categorisation in respect of values, personality and beliefs, tied to brands, product and services.)

Although this breakdown of segmentation criteria is fairly elementary in relation to the complexity of the models currently developed, it nevertheless provides a clear distinction between public, private and personal information. Gender, ethnicity, social status and, in general, information required for social interaction are mainly public. Behavioural patterns may reveal personal, privacy-relevant information, but usually pertain to individual choices of no interest to the rest of the community. Psychographic-oriented information is privacy-related.

---

[7] Barrie Gunter, *The Psychology of Consumer Profiling in a Digital Age* (*Routledge Studies in Marketing*) (London: Taylor and Francis, 2010) 7.

My values, my faith and my beliefs are just mine. I can interact with the outside world without revealing them, therefore nobody should be permitted surreptitiously to invade my *sancta santorum* and remove such personal information:

> An individual's personality reveals more about their character than simply knowing the type of lifestyle they lead or the cultural values they hold most dear ... The distinctive way each of us responds in a specific situation differentiates us from other people. If we display consistency in the way we respond to a specific situation, this could be because we have been hardwired to react in a particular way.[8]

As much as this may sound like a novel theory, it amounts to little more than a revamped version of 1960s 'Psycho-Cybernetics',[9] a syncretic approach to human behaviour modification based on the early research on cybernetics by John Von Neumann[10] and Norbert Wiener,[11] blended with cognitive behavioural techniques.

Cognitive behavioural techniques, though, are not the only ones to be exploited in psychometric research, for many different psychological or psychoanalytic approaches have been attempted in order better to X-ray the individual's mind. But the overwhelming role and quantity of individual-related data collected online is based on a (marketing-oriented) longstanding ideological assumption: humans are living machines, and machines can be programmed to react to stimuli in an almost deterministic way.

The intrinsic limit of such models, however, has always been the lack of a statistically-sound data set in respect of both quantity and quality, as well as the possibility of obtaining 'direct access' to consumers' minds in order to establish what individuals really do think:

> There are many factors that have drawn marketers to online data analytics ... There is no direct data collection cost involved ... The online consumer data are generated naturally and do not involve an intervention in consumers' lives ... the sheer scale of online data collection ... cannot usually be matched by offline research because it would be far too costly to contemplate.[12]

It was therefore rather obvious that the growth of the networked part of people's daily lives would present an enormous opportunity to refine individual behaviour studies. But how exactly is this online information exploited by profiling?

> There are two aspects of consumer segmentation grounded in psychological variables that will be considered in the context of the digital media ... The first ... comprises a form of 'behavioural segmentation' based on the online behavioural activities of consumers.

---

[8] Barrie Gunter, ibid, 29.

[9] Maxwell Maltz, *Psycho-Cybernetics* (New York: Simon & Schuster, 1960).

[10] John Von Neumann, 'The General and Logical Theory of Automata' in LA Jeffress (ed), *Cerebral Mechanisms in Behavior: The Hixon Symposium* (New York: John Wiley & Sons, 1951) 1–31.

[11] Norbert Wiener, *Cybernetics: Or Control and Communication in the Animal and the Machine* (Paris: Hermann & Cie Paris, 1948).

[12] Barrie Gunter, ibid, 19.

The second ... entails the use of psychographic measures, including personality traits originally developed outside consumer contexts, to explain online behaviour.[13]

This may suggest that myriad panopticons' adepts are controlling our activities online. But the reality is rather different. Common profiling methods sold to the majority of businesses either simply do not work or are of limited efficacy and, as will be suggested below, privacy is threatened by the new methods of manufacturing political consent rather than by a horde of 'serial profilers' in the digital wild.

To illustrate this point, suppose that, for a few years, you use Amazon or Google (including Gmail, YouTube, Google docs and the rest of the package) with your privacy settings entirely switched off. What happens? Will you receive 'personalised' recommendations? Or will you, in fact, receive the same 'benefits' that immediately change when you search for something other than your usual search?

Moreover, are the results of your searches any better? Or are you just shown 'relevant' content, classified as such because of the topic and not because of its informative value? Is it possible that all the effort and the spin put into big data, machine learning, 'artificial intelligence', and so on do little more than provide information on cheap hardware tools produced by a Far Eastern manufacturer? Should we not trust our direct experience? If so, we are driven to conclude that 'Internet profiling' is like the Arabian Phoenix invoked by the Italian poet Pietro Metastasio: '*che ci sia ciascun lo dice, dove sia nessun lo sa*': 'everybody says it does exist, but nobody ever saw it.'

Of course, the web is replete with software and platforms that promise 'insightful information about users' or 'highly effective business intelligence tools' or 'top-notch analytics'. But one detail is often overlooked: the fact that such services/products are based on a sales pitch that entails the dubious quid pro quo: 'we give you the tools; you bring the data, the algorithm and the database queries.'

Sometimes, as in the case of the computing facilities offered by Amazon Web Services, this is clearly stated; in other situations this is not so apparent, and the 'wannabe-profiler' is lured into thinking that by putting a few JavaScript lines on his or her pages, or allowing the 'analytics provider' to access his mostly ignored website, he or she will be able to collect personal information about perfect strangers. The truth is that there is a difference, in terms of resources, quantity and quality of data, between what digital robber barons collect and what is collected by (or given to) the myriad 'marketing experts' and managers. In other words, the digital robber barons (and their close associates) have sufficient information to exploit as behaviour analysis and prediction according to their mysterious algorithms. The rest of the world, simply, does not.

Thus if the vast quantities of information collected are of some use, at least in respect of sales of data and/or analytics, to companies of every size, the further you are from data-driven businesses, the more the 'profiling reliability' and related privacy concerns become a myth. 'Analytics' of various kinds are currently used by

---

[13] ibid, 175.

(and, therefore, sold to) companies of very different sizes: from small family-run businesses to multinational retail corporations, from pipe manufacturers to craft beer brewers. But, notwithstanding the size of the company that purchases these tools, the amount of information has not been proven to be useful because of its limited intrinsic value. Well-known, multinational-owned brands, sold through the large distribution channels such as shopping malls and department stores, invest huge sums of money annually to obtain consumers' data.

'Co-branding' website initiatives, mall-collected coupons, or online fidelity clubs are but a few of the multitude of activities conducted simply to acquire thousands of email addresses or telephone numbers to occasionally stalk victims with offers and surveys. There is no profiling, no 'hidden processing', and no 'fishbowl-swimming consumer' being constantly monitored. The overriding effect of these endeavours is to increase the rate at which spam clogs the arteries of the Internet. The final scene of *The Internship* vividly captures this phenomenon. The 2013 film relates the story of a couple of middle-aged sales representatives who, after having being fired by their company, try to re-invent themselves by attending an internship-competition at Google. Teams of young talents are summoned to Google's headquarters. Following a summer ordeal of seminars and trials, only one team will be hired. The winning team must then attempt to sell Google's services to the owner of a pizzeria who initially turned down the offer to expand his business through the platform. He is persuaded by 'analytics' showing that there are people interested in his pizza from neighbouring cities, and by having found a possible location for a second pizzeria close to a fresh goods market where he can replicate his 'business model' based on purchasing daily fresh ingredients. The team's 'closing argument' is along these lines:

> [N]ew customers, new franchise, and that's just the tip of the iceberg … it's all waiting at the click of a button … everybody is searching for something … they're searching for you. We just wanna help them find you.

Although this 'pizza shop sales pitch' is regarded as an excellent way to demonstrate the 'power of (Google) analytics', it actually fails. If the outcome of Google's extensive profiling activity was merely a list of anonymous people from a few small towns craving a slice of pizza, that would be of no interest to a privacy-concerned citizen. But the business and politics industry of consent manufacturing, active in the United States at least since the beginning of the twentieth century, has far more ambitious objectives; it seeks to influence our behaviour by influencing our thoughts. And to do so it aggressively harvests not only private information about our social interactions, but also intimate personal information.

IV. Privacy and Pollsters

Long before the rise of the digital robber barons, the history of American pollsters reveals a clear evolutionary path pursued by the data-driven sector. At the very beginning, when technical, logistical and mathematical limitations made it diffi-cult to analyse huge quantities of information, the chief methods were the 'sample quota' approach (discussed below). Privacy was not at stake because the informa-tion came from voluntary interviews with a limited number of persons.

In less than a century, though, the position underwent a profound change; the consent-manufacturing machine began to use information about people obtained from third parties. This information was sometimes innocuous; more often it carried a threat of danger, although it was not in itself dangerous.

At first blush, there is no direct relationship between the right to privacy and the pollsters' activities devoted to predicting the outcome of a political contest, or suggesting the optimum strategy to engage voters. But matters are not so straightforward. Recent developments in political campaigning have altered the traditional approach. From pure 'electoral crystal balls', these machines have been transformed into 'consent moulders'. And in this exercise a particularly valuable resource is that which can be extracted from personal information.

Long before Google, the most successful example of predicting future devel-opments using data and mathematics was the 1936 forecast of the election of Roosevelt as President. This prediction established the American Institute of Public Opinion (later re-named 'Gallup') in the empyrean of 'fortune tellers'.[14] Its approach was based on the method of 'quota sampling'[15] applied to (relatively) small but statistically superior selected samples of 50,000 respondents, while their competitor, the *Literary Digest*, relied upon its 10 million-member mailing list, assembled from various sources, but targeting the middle and upper classes, to obtain a population of 2.4 million respondents. Unlike Gallup, the *Literary Digest* failed to provide a reliable forecast as its approach suffered from two flaws. First, 'selection bias' (the chosen group of participants failed to account for the whole strata of society), and secondly, the 'non response bias' (it took into account only a few answers to the poll.)

The *Literary Digest* fiasco refutes the conclusion that the larger the sample, the more accurate the prediction.[16] But the quota sampling method was not free of its own drawbacks. Gallup again succeeded in correctly predicting the outcome of both the 1940 and 1944 presidential elections. In 1948, however, in not predicting

[14] Of the three pollsters that analysed the US elections – George Gallup, Elmo Roper and Archibald Crossey – only the first actually publicised his prediction; the others did not survey voters' inten-tions, but merely their guesses about the likely winner. See Susan Ohmer, *George Gallup in Hollywood* (New York: Columbia University Press, 2006) 62.

[15] Under a quota-controlled sample, the survey researcher sought to interview predetermined proportions of people from particular segments of society. The researcher controlled this process by dividing, or 'stratifying', the population into a number of mutually exclusive subpopulations (or strata) thought to capture politically relevant divisions (such as gender and region). Researchers then allocated the sample among these strata in proportion to their desired size. See Adam J Berinsky, 'American Public Opinion in 1930 and 1940: The Analysis of Quota-controlled Sample Survey Data' (2006) 70(4) *Public Opinion Quarterly* 499.

[16] https://www.math.upenn.edu/~deturck/m170/wk4/lecture/case1.html (visited 15 August 2018).

the return of the Democrat President Harry Truman for a second term, it suffered a major failure, rooted in the weakness of the quota sampling's rationale:

> The basic idea of quota sampling is on the surface a good one: Force the sample to be a representative cross-section of the population … Right away we can see one of the potential problems: Where do we stop? No matter how careful one might be, there is always the possibility that some criterion that would affect the way people vote might be missed and the sample could be deficient in this regard.[17]

But if this is correct, how did Gallup correctly predict the result of the previous elections? It was probably due to a combination of the human factor and good luck. Gallup's field researchers decided who should be interviewed, and by examining the responses ex post facto, they overestimated the extent of the Republican vote. In the previous elections 'the spread between the candidates was large enough to cover the error. In 1948 Gallup, and all the other pollsters, simply ran out of luck.'[18]

Obviously the models used to analyse human behaviour have become considerably more complex and sophisticated, but this brief account of the rise of the profiling business supports the idea that no matter how sound a model may be, whenever humans are involved in selecting the sample, bias inevitably creeps in. In the words of Edward Bernays, 'the father of public relations':

> The conscious and intelligent manipulation of the organized habits and opinions of the masses is an important element in democratic society. Those who manipulate this unseen mechanism of society constitute an invisible government which is the true ruling power of our country … We are governed, our minds are molded, our tastes formed, our ideas suggested, largely by men we have never heard of.[19]

Bernays was one of these men. Ethical questions aside, he succeeded in shaping the conscience of Americans to match those of his 'clients': private companies, lobbyists and even the US government. Long before the Internet, search engines, and social networking hysteria, he was well aware of the role of 'wireless' communication technology as a tool to shape personal ideas and beliefs:

> The groupings and affiliations of society to-day are no longer subject to 'local and sectional' limitations. When the Constitution was adopted, the unit of organization was the village community, which … generated its group ideas and opinions by personal contact and discussion directly among its citizens. But to-day, because ideas can be instantaneously transmitted to any distance and to any number of people, this geographical integration has been supplemented by many other kinds of grouping, so that persons having the same ideas and interests may be associated and regimented for common action even though they live thousands of miles apart.[20]

---

[17] Dennis de Turck: https://www.math.upenn.edu/~deturck/m170/wk4/lecture/case2.html (visited 15 August 2018).

[18] https://www.math.upenn.edu/~deturck/m170/wk4/lecture/case2.html (visited 15 August 2018).

[19] Edward Bernays, *Propaganda* (New York: Horace Liveright Inc, 1928) 9.

[20] ibid, 13.

Written in 1928, these prescient words describe our contemporary 'interconnected world'. And they expose the main illusion that the digital robber barons are selling, with personal information being the currency to pay the price of a ploy that does not exist for the average company: 'personalisation'.

While, as Bernays demonstrated, it is possible to achieve a certain degree of, as he put it, 'group regimentation', this cannot occur in a deterministic way or, in particular, on an individual basis – at least not for every kind of company that buys a $100-per-year profiling package on the web. There are, of course, major developments in this field, including, as the 2012 Obama campaign demonstrated, 'micro-targeting' which advances the prospect of an individualised approach, rejecting the 'traditional' manner of classifying individuals by age, gender, geography and so on under an updated and revised version of the 'quota sampling' approach:

> Instead, the electorate could be seen as a collection of individual citizens who could each be measured and assessed on their own terms. Now it was up to a candidate who wanted to lead those people to build a campaign that would interact with them the same way.[21]

This is precisely what Bernays wrote about the influence of wireless communication in the shaping of individual beliefs. The pendulum is swinging backwards, from the attempt to treat humans as faceless cogs in a complex, soulless machine, to the handling of (relatively) small crowds of people sharing common, localised sets of beliefs, using an army of volunteers that, following the carefully drafted individual profiles, attempts to win the hearts of the electorate.

In other words, the Obama campaign reinforced the importance of the human factor. The utilisation of vast quantities of personal data was a key factor in winning the election. But that was just a part, albeit a significant one, of the strategy which would not have worked well without the ability to analyse in (almost) real time voters' feedback, adapt 'the message' to be delivered, and train the volunteers to deliver the refined outcome.

This brief account of the consent-manufacturing world illustrates that to make sense of data, especially in large amounts, one requires a profound grasp of statistics, sociology, economics, politics, psychology and database programming and, above all, significant financial resources.

The 'benefit' that an ordinary business (such as the pizzeria in *The Internship*) acquires from these profiling services is merely raw data which, although packaged in glossy envelopes, is actually classified in old-fashioned, predetermined frameworks that blend 'objective' information such as age-range or gender with partial assumptions such as 'interest' and 'category'.

---

[21] Sasha Issenberg, 'How Obama's Team Used Big Data to Rally Voters', *MIT Technology Review*, 19 December 2012: https://www.technologyreview.com/s/509026/how-obamas-team-used-big-data-to-rally-voters/ (visited 16 August 2018).

What specific dangers does profiling pose to the right to privacy? The answer resides, again, in the fundamental distinction between 'private life' and 'privacy'. As soon as we express an idea, a political belief, or allegiance to a religious creed, we are choosing to transfer this information from the secret chest that protects our inner self to a non-secret (but still 'private') social and legal space in which the persona[22] we choose to assume allows us to play our selected role in society and thereby interact with others.

The idea that an individual can be more than a single character during his daily life – a core to the right of privacy in the sense that allows us to remove our social mask[23] – is not confined to Western society.

In Japan, for instance, while a privacy debate arose only in 1964 following the Tokyo District Court decision in the 宴のあと (*Utage no Ato*) case,[24] a distinction has long been drawn between various circles of relationships with different levels of 'openness' toward others, beginning with 'real intention', 本音 *Honne*, to 'public stance' て前 *Tatemae*, as opposed to private thoughts,

> The sphere of the inner self is called 私 (*Watashi*) which means either 'I' or 'private'. The first 'external' contact is with family 身内 (*Miuchi*) and then, gradually, the flow of relationships proceeds toward being part of a group, 内 *Uchi*, interaction with people connected with a group 内外 (*Naigai*), outside a group 外 (*Soto*) and finally with unrelated people 他人 (*Tanin*).[25] In this regard, though, while in Japan privacy as a legal matter emerged only in the mid-1960s,[26] at a social level there was already a clear perception of the difference between private and public dimensions.

The Japanese approach to privacy is interesting because even though there had been the possibility to recognise privacy as an autonomous right appealing to the country's social customs, law-makers left this to the judiciary, and focused on the protection of personal information[27] from big data misuse[28] rather than on threats

---

[22] In Roman Law, the term '*persona*', inspired by the Greek word '*prosôpon*' – a theatrical mask – had two different meanings: '*persona*' as a universal concept, and '*persona*' as a character, playing several different roles in society. See Francesco Viola, 'Lo statuto giuridico della persona in prospettiva storica' in Gustavo Pansini (ed), *Studi in memoria di Italo Mancini* (Naples: Edizioni Scientifiche Italiane, 1999) 621–41.

[23] Raymond Wacks, *Privacy: A Very Short Introduction*, 2nd edn (Oxford: Oxford University Press, 2015) 38. See generally Erving Goffman, *The Presentation of Self in Everyday Life* (London: Penguin, 1990).

[24] 宴のあと (*Utage no Ato*) is a novel by the famous Japanese writer 三島 由紀夫 (Mishima Yukio), published in 1960, where the author recounts a private conversation with the politician 有田 八郎 (Arita Hachiro), who then sued the writer for infringement of his privacy.

[25] Andrew Adams, Kiyoshi Murata and Yohko Orito, 'The Japanese Sense of Information Privacy' in (2009) 24(4) *AI & Society* 327–41.

[26] More precisely, according the Japanese calendar, Year 39 of 昭和時代, *Showa Era*.

[27] See Hiroshi Miyashita, 'The Evolving Concept of Data Privacy in Japanese Law' (2011) 1(4) *International Data Privacy Law* 229.

[28] The first case, in 2013, involved the exploitation for marketing purposes of more than 4 million debit card numbers used on the train and underground, to promote nearby commercial outlets. The second case, in 2014, related to the hidden, and then suspended, face recognition system experiment at Osaka station. The third, in the same year, concerned the sale of some 48 million personal data records

to individuals. While the Japanese legal notion of privacy suffers from the same 'identity crisis' as its Western counterpart, the social sense of privacy reinforces the idea that the need to be in control of one's own intimate, personal information is common to all human beings, along with the right to display to our family, our acquaintances, and others with whom we interact, the social role we choose to reveal. We create a profile of ourselves and circumscribe a personal space in which we exercise control over the personal information we decide to reveal. Thus, once we relinquish this control, there is progressively less privacy at stake.

Again, the analysis of the second Obama campaign's use of data to maximise the efficacy of the political message is revealing. In the quest to determine how better to exploit television broadcasting to reach potential voters, data scientists discovered that they were unable to intersect the information amassed about voters with the information owned by cable TV stations. To solve this problem, they devised a scheme whereby research firms repackaged their data in a form that would allow the campaign to access the individual histories without infringing the cable providers' privacy standards:

> [T]he campaign provided a list of persuadable voters and their addresses, derived from its micro-targeting models, and the [Rentrak] company looked for them in the cable providers' billing files. When a record matched, Rentrak would issue it a unique household ID that identified viewing data from a single set-top box but masked any personally identifiable information.[29]

This is a clear example of what happens when the two dimensions of privacy and private life collide, with undesirable unforeseen casualties. One's political or personal views expressed *publicly*, while still part of a private dimension, do not qualify for protection in the name of privacy. Tracking who knows who, or who does what and where and to whom – as typically occurs on social networking platforms – may raise concerns of personal safety, free speech, or global surveillance; but not in respect of control over personal information. *Voce dal sen fuggita, poi richiamar non vale.*[30]

By contrast, the viewing/listening/reading choices of an individual patently belong to the private realm. But it is surely the case that that we forfeit privacy when we are compelled to disclose our personal information to access streamed contents such as films or music, or to read e-books, and the information is recorded on centralised systems. As soon as we connect to these services, we have already informed Netflix or Spotify of our preferences and when we like to 'enjoy' them. And this is equally true of Kindle, and other e-books. They intrude upon our intimate selves.

---

in the education sector to three data brokers. Hiroshi Myashita, 'Data Protection Laws in Japan' in Gloria González Fuster, Rosamunde van Brakel, Paul De Hert (eds), *Research Handbook on Privacy and Data Protection Law: Values, Norms and Global Politics* (Cheltenham: Edward Elgar, forthcoming).
[29] Sasha Issenberg, ibid.
[30] 'A word spoken cannot be taken back,' Metastasio in his 1744 opera, *Ipermestra*.

My LinkedIn or Facebook persona might be genuine, slightly doctored, or entirely misleading, if not completely false. But which books I read, the music I listen to, and the movies I watch do provide actual intimate information, as do my Google searches. Therefore, since my ideas and beliefs are among my most intimate types of personal information that shape my social being, gaining access to them is an invasion of privacy, especially when the object is to use this information to manipulate my life.

This explains why the costly and complex legal and technically convoluted solutions that allowed Obama's data scientists to 'access the individual histories without violating the cable providers' privacy standards' are simply a smoke screen to conceal the fact that voters' privacy has been violated as soon as the results of these activities allowed the individualisation of the political message to be delivered, and the will of the voters 'controlled'.

The position is little different in the pursuit of 'pure' marketing goals. Digital robber barons might have different views about the role of privacy in their business model, but privacy is nevertheless implicated. In general, their attitude towards privacy may be summarised in three-plus-one approaches:

1. We don't actually care about privacy (Facebook);[31]
2. We pretend to care, while we actually don't (Google);[32]
3. We do care, because we don't want to be involved in user-generated quarrels; we sell our products by appearing to champion privacy.[33] But we might change our mind if business requests it.[34] (Apple).

The third-plus one is the Amazon approach: We process an enormous quantity of actual privacy-related information, and we succeed in ensuring that nobody actually cares about how we deal with privacy issues, because we 'just' want to sell goods in the best way possible, by incorporating human behaviour analysis in our sales practices.

But what is omitted – and this is the fundamental privacy issue – is the cultural shift in both the business and consumer realms that the digital robber barons have been able to start. Virtually every company, no matter how small, deludes itself into believing that they can 'make sense' out of human behaviour. And, in general, consumers do not object to exchanging their public, private, and personal

---

[31] Bobbie Johnson, 'Privacy no longer a social norm, says Facebook founder', *The Guardian*: https://www.theguardian.com/technology/2010/jan/11/facebook-privacy.

[32] Richard Esguerra, 'Google CEO Eric Schmidt Dismisses the Importance of Privacy', 10 December 2009: https://www.eff.org/deeplinks/2009/12/google-ceo-eric-schmidt-dismisses-privacy (visited 28 August 2018).

[33] Tim Cook, 'A Message to Our Customers', 16 February 2016: https://www.apple.com/customer-letter/ (visited 28 August 2018).

[34] Amnesty International, 'Campaign targets Apple over privacy betrayal for Chinese iCloud users': https://www.amnesty.org/en/latest/news/2018/03/apple-privacy-betrayal-for-chinese-icloud-users/ (visited 28 August 2018).

information for worthless trade-offs, yet they protest when somebody gazes into their backyard, no matter how exposed to public view it is. And, far worse, lawmakers and data protection commissioners seem to have fallen into this very same cultural trap.

In other words, as mentioned in Chapter one, outside the academic and professional legal community, a different sense of privacy prevails. It matters not whether I am in my home with the curtains closed or crossing the crowded Shibuya intersection in Tokyo; nobody should be entitled to merely to stare casually at me. It is immaterial whether my comment was made on a public online forum or that I sent a strongly encrypted email to a correspondent; in both cases my messages are 'confidential'. I want to be free to tag whoever comes within reach of my mouse, but I complain when somebody does the same to me. I know I can pay less for a product if I subscribe to an 'online user club', but then I fulminate because of the 'promotional messages' I receive as a result.

Is this schizophrenic and arbitrary attitude toward our (digital) life the privacy we are striving to protect? Is this genuinely 'privacy'? Or is it actually concealment, confidentiality, and secrecy? Is it no more than a desire to be free from prying eyes to do what we wish?

5

Personal Information and Freedom

I. Introduction

In 1755 Benjamin Franklin famously wrote to the Governor of Pennsylvania:[1]

> Those who would give up essential Liberty, to purchase a little temporary Safety, deserve neither Liberty nor Safety.

His statement has been widely misunderstood:

> Franklin was writing not as a subject being asked to cede his liberty to government, but in his capacity as a legislator being asked to renounce his power to tax lands notionally under his jurisdiction. In other words, the 'essential liberty' to which Franklin referred was thus not what we would think of today as civil liberties but, rather, the right of self-governance of a legislature in the interests of collective security.[2]

For example, prominent privacy scholar and leading international cryptography expert, Bruce Schneier, dubbed a 'security guru' by *The Economist*, has written:

> If you set up the false dichotomy, of course people will choose security over privacy – especially if you scare them first. But it's still a false dichotomy. There is no security without privacy. And liberty requires both security and privacy. The famous quote attributed to Benjamin Franklin reads: 'Those who would give up essential liberty to purchase a little temporary safety, deserve neither liberty nor safety.' It's also true that those who would give up privacy for security are likely to end up with neither.[3]

He misconceives the meaning of this celebrated declaration in a number of respects. First, it is founded on what Franklin regarded as the 'wrong' kind of liberty (individual freedom rather than that of a political institution). Secondly, Schneier overlooks the adjectives and adverbs that qualify and modify the key words in Franklin's postulate, namely 'essential' liberty, 'a little temporary' safety.

---

[1] Benjamin Franklin, *Pennsylvania Assembly: Reply to the Governor* in *Votes and Proceedings of the House of Representatives, 1755–1756* (Philadelphia PA, 1756) 19–21, available online at: https://founders.archives.gov/documents/Franklin/01-06-02-0107 (visited 4 December 2018).

[2] Benjamin Wittes, *What Ben Franklin Really Said*: https://www.lawfareblog.com/what-ben-franklin-really-said (visited 4 December 2018).

[3] Bruce Schneier, 'What Our Top Spy Doesn't Get: Security and Privacy Aren't Opposites', *Wired.com* online edition, 24 January 2008, available at: https://www.wired.com/2008/01/securitymatters-0124/ (visited 4 December 2018).

Thirdly, the relativity of Franklin's words is turned into an absolute.[4] Finally, where Franklin writes 'safety', Schneier – and many who blindly invoke Benjamin Franklin as a 'privacy champion' – reads 'security' as computer security: a horse of a different colour.

Furthermore, the verbatim text of Franklin's assertion may be rephrased as 'essential liberty can be sacrificed to purchase substantial safety.' This semantic permutation would still – paradoxically – be valid from Franklin's perspective, but its application to Schneier's claim demonstrates his error.

How are we to measure how likely is the 'likely' that Schneier mentions? Who should set the limit? And at what level of intrusiveness into the privacy of an individual? Moreover, Schneier's corollary to Franklin's Law is based on the assumption that 'liberty requires both security and privacy'. But this is not what Franklin wrote; he puts liberty in one corner and safety in another – without mentioning security at all![5] What 'liberty' is being described? And what species of 'privacy'? Are safety and security interchangeable concepts?

To draw on an historical example, ordinary Italians who survived the Second World War and who had no actual political engagement with Mussolini's regime, when recalling this period, often say: 'we felt safe', 'we could leave the key in the door, or the bicycle unchained and still be sure that nothing would happen.' Were they 'safe'? Were they 'free'? Was their 'privacy' protected? Public policy of a dictatorial regime clearly seeks to preserve its existence, but may, as a by-product, guarantee a certain amount of public safety from (minor) crimes and other threats.

The Iron Curtain Era provides countless examples of how safety was disconnected from liberty. One instance will suffice:

> The welfare state of East German socialism had two sides to it. Social policy was the carrot alongside the stick of repression. It was both the counterpart and the complement of the police state. This constellation was not entirely new. But the especially remarkable thing about the GDR was that the introduction and expansion of social policy coincided with an equally energetic introduction and expansion of a mammoth apparatus for observation and repression.[6]

Even in an authoritarian regime, individuals stay safe, and 'enjoy' (different levels of) liberty and a certain degree of protection for the intimacy of life that was not necessarily banned even under limited conditions of liberty.

---

[4] The argument has been raised in Eugene Volokh, 'Liberty, safety and Benjamin Franklin', *The Washington Post* online edition, 11 November 2014: https://www.washingtonpost.com/news/volokh-conspiracy/wp/2014/11/11/liberty-safety-and-benjamin-franklin/?noredirect=on&utm_term=.de62d9303979 visited 4 December 2018.

[5] For the sake of the argument, we may add that if liberty = privacy + security, then privacy = liberty – security.

[6] Manfred G Schmidt, 'Social Policy in the German Democratic Republic' in Manfred G Schmidt and Gerhard A Ritter, *The Rise and Fall of a Socialist Welfare State: The German Democratic Republic (1949–1990) and German Unification (1989–1994)* (Berlin: Springer, 2012) 130.

It may seem counterintuitive, but the Italian Penal Code passed in the Fascist period, and which remains in force, accorded considerable protection to personal and family life. This protection was so strong that incest was not considered a criminal offence in itself, but only when it caused 'public scandal'. This is because Section 564 of the Penal Code, a provision that lasted well after the fall of Mussolini's regime, stipulated that incest was a crime against morality and not a crime against the person. Therefore – and this is not meant frivolously – if the prohibited behaviour took place behind closed doors, no offence would have been committed. In the course of the debate in 1930 that reached this conclusion, it was argued:

> The danger of giving way to investigations within families is great, because of the dire consequences that might be provoked. There would be a mortal blow to public morals ... On the other hand ... in Italy incest is not that frequent, therefore a balance must be struck between the concerns for the decadence of the race, on the one hand, and the no less deserving consideration of avoiding scandalous investigations into the intimacy of family life, on the other.[7]

Democratic societies are no less susceptible to distortions in the application of putative 'privacy' (or data) protection. Spain's constitutional crisis of September 2017, when the autonomous region of Catalonia declared its independence from Madrid, demonstrates how data protection may be used to suppress freedom. When Catalonian leaders sought to access the electoral lists to organise the separatist referendum, the Spanish Data Protection Authority warned that such a move would be an infringement of the GDPR, while the Catalonian Data Protection Authority claimed that the use of personal data for this purpose was legitimate. Whatever the correct interpretation, it is plain that both data protection authorities deliberately entered a purely political battle in a partisan way, using personal data protection as a means to curtail the political rights of the citizens or, from another perspective, to contribute to a constitutional coup.[8]

On 12 November 2018 the European Commission warned Romania not to use the General Data Protection Regulation (GDPR) to threaten freedom of the press.[9] The Romanian Data Protection Authority had asked a journalist to disclose his sources. A week later, the European Digital Rights Initiative (EDRI) and other NGOs involved in digital rights protection wrote to the chair of the European Data Protection Board to denounce this peculiar 'enforcement' of the Data Protection Regulation.[10]

---

[7] David Brunelli, 'Incesto' in *Trattato di diritto penale – parte speciale. Delitti contro la famiglia*, Volume 4 (Milan: Giuffrè, 2011). English translation by Andrea Monti.

[8] 'Spain's Data Protection Agency warns polling supervisors of fines of up to €300,000', *Catalan News*, 29 September 2017: http://www.catalannews.com/politics/item/spain-s-data-protection-agency-warns-polling-supervisors-of-fines-of-up-to-300000 (visited 10 December 2018).

[9] Nikolaj Nielsen, 'EU warns Romania not to abuse GDPR against press', *EU Observer*, 12 November 2018: https://euobserver.com/justice/143356 (visited 10 December 2018).

[10] EDRI et al, *Misuse of GDPR threatens media freedom in Romania*: https://www.apti.ro/sites/default/files/ApTI%20and%20PI%20letter%20to%20EDPB%20-%20RISE%20Project.pdf (visited 9 December 2018).

The Spanish and Romanian Data Protection Authorities are not alone in expanding the reach of data protection legislation. In fact, Italy came first in this race; in October 2006, enforcing its data protection code, the Italian authority blocked the broadcasting of an investigation into the use of drugs by Italian MPs by a renowned television programme:

> Some MPs have been subjected, unbeknown to them, to a simple test that reveals the recent use of drugs.[11] The percentage of 'positives' is impressive. The experiment was conducted in a way that no one, not even the authors of the show, can know to whom the 'swabs' are connected: anonymous data, therefore, that make the censorship intervention of the Authority for the protection of personal data very questionable.[12]

Treating data protection as a synonym for privacy, by linking the latter to other rights, creates confusion and leads to paradoxical and contradictory results. Both examples, diametrically opposed, demonstrate that there is no necessary connection between privacy and security.

Moreover, as previously argued, the tendency to regard privacy as parasitic upon, or even indistinguishable from, associated rights such as secrecy or confidentiality strips the right to privacy of its essence. And it raises the question why, if such rights provide adequate protection, is the right to privacy required at all?

Law-abiding citizens are entitled to expect a democratic state to respect their right not to be placed under such unnecessary surveillance so as to limit the free exercise of political and civil rights. Equally, they have the right not to be subjected to unauthorised intrusions into their non-public and family life. The Italian Penal Code, for example, in Article 615 *bis* ('unlawful invasion of private life'), criminalises newsgathering by way of audio, photographic or video equipment which targets an individual's private domicile and, in Article 615 *ter* ('unauthorised access to a computer or telecommunications system'), accessing a person's computer that the law protects as one's 'digital domicile'.

This protection differs from that sought by the leader of a drug cartel, an unfaithful partner, or a human rights activist. They seek, not the legal right to privacy, but secrecy or anonymity in order to safeguard their covert activities from exposure.

II. Anonymity

To illustrate the misconception, consider the case of anon.penet.fi, the Finnish pseudonymous remailer launched in 1993 which was shut down three years later after a series of legal battles.

---

[11] Pretending to prepare the MP for the interview, the host of the show had the make-up-man brush a cotton swab over the interviewee's forehead; he then discarded the swab in a canister, together with the others without labelling it. The sweat absorbed by the swabs was then tested for drugs and the result would have been presented in the TV show 'Le Iene'.

[12] Manlio Cammarata, 'Libertà di informazione e diritto di sapere', *Interlex*, 12 October 2006: http://www.interlex.it/675/leiene.htm (visited 9 December 2018). English translation by Andrea Monti.

In 1993 a Finnish Internet Service Provider, Johan Helsingius, devised and made available on the Internet the very first pseudonymous remailer server. The system was so designed to provide users with an email address under the 'anon. penet.fi' domain, such as johndoe@anon.penet.it, which was used as a public front-end in newsgroup posting. Users were able to post and receive messages on the Usenet (the early internet public discussion platform) without revealing their identity, which was known only to the server administrator (Helsingius himself).

Helsingius was dubbed a 'privacy prophet'[13] and his remailer was immediately enlisted in the 'privacy protection arsenal': 'Privacy advocates applauded Helsingius for starting the first easy-to-use remailer. In their eyes, it was a rare expansion of rights in an age marked by narrowing.'[14] His purpose, however, had little to do with privacy, and everything to do with the exercise of free speech. As he put it: '[T]he original idea was just to prove a point, to prove that you can't censor anything on the Internet because there is always a technological solution to circumvent any political or whatever censorship.'[15]

But Helsingius' free-speech wall lasted less than a couple of years. In February 1995 the Church of Scientology reported to Interpol the unlawful dissemination of copyrighted files by a Penet user, and was able to obtain a warrant compelling Helsingius to disclose the real e-mail address of the alleged infringer. History was repeated on 22 September 1996 when – once again – in legal proceedings involving Penet, the Finnish Court of Appeal ordered Helsingius to release the identity of a user who – once again – was accused of publicising Scientology's confidential documents. Three days later *The Observer* depicted Helsingius as 'the Internet middleman who handles 90 per cent of all child pornography'.[16]

This allegation was untrue:

> The American police officer quoted in that account has since said that he was misquoted, and that very little child porn is sent through remailers. Helsingius had worked with a Finnish police officer to prevent child pornographers from using his service, in part by limiting the size of messages below the size of most photos.[17]

The pressure on Helsingius nevertheless proved intolerable, and he decided to abandon his anonymous – or more accurately, pseudonymous – remailing service.

---

[13] Jessie Scanlon, 'Anon.penet.fi RIP', *Wired* online edition, 11 January 1996: https://www.wired.com/1996/11/anon-penet-fi-rip/ (visited 28 December 2018).

[14] John Schwartz, 'Networkings: With e-mail privacy in jeopardy, "remailer" closes up shop', *The Washington Post* online edition, 16 September 1996, available at: https://www.washingtonpost.com/archive/business/1996/09/16/with-e-mail-privacy-in-jeopardy-remailer-closes-up-shop/64c912d9-50e2-46e0-9dec-4a62c94a9f70/ (visited 27 December 2018.)

[15] Volker Grassmuck, 'Don't Try to Control the Network Because it's Impossible Anyway', *IC Magazine*, NTT Publishing, 12/94, available at: http://waste.informatik.hu-berlin.de/~grassmuck/Texts/remailer.html (visited 27 December 2018).

[16] Jessie Scanlon, *Wired*, n 13 above.

[17] John Schwartz, *The Washington Post*, n 14 above.

In other words, this case demonstrates how a clash between free speech and copyright, along with unfounded allegations of child pornography facilitation led to the closure of anon.penet.fi. But it also generated considerable discussion of the consequences of the closure of the service. It sparked a debate between Esther Dyson, then chairperson of the US NGO the Electronic Frontier Foundation, and a then unknown activist, Julian Assange. Addressing Assange's criticism about being shocked by Dyson's position on the Helsingius case, she wrote:

> Anonymity can be dangerous – as can traceability, especially in/by repressive regimes. Therefore I would favor allowing anonymity – with some form of traceability only under terms considerably stronger than what are generally required for a wiretap. Anyone who seriously needs anonymity because of a repressive government is likely to use a foreign (outside whatever jurisdiction he fears) server, so that this is not a matter of 'local' laws. The tracer would have to pass through what I hope would be tighter hoops than we have now.[18]

Dyson's interpretation of Assange's argument is revealing; she acknowledges, first, that anonymity is a factual condition that does not necessarily imply the existence of a right to privacy and, secondly, that a right to privacy is not required to establish anonymity as a factual condition. But more important is when she elucidates her position: 'Please note that this is not the same as the right to *private* conversations and the use of encryption; this is the issue of being accountable for what you publish in public.'[19]

The apex of this controversy is still to be reached. The evolution of pseudonymous remailers into actual anonymous message platforms, and the spreading of blockchain-based applications (mainly, cryptocurrencies) raise novel questions whose answers suggest that they have little connection to the right to privacy.

Recently, *Der Spiegel* and *La Repubblica* exclusively published the contents of files acquired anonymously from WikiLeaks that revealed secret information about the United States' operations in the Middle East.[20] There is no evidence of a quid pro quo in this transaction, but it is highly improbable that WikiLeaks could grant such an exclusive without some form of compensation.

Were the information obtained directly by journalists, no problem would have arisen. As soon as information arrives on a journalist's desk the only question is 'Am I still on time to meet the paper's deadline?' When, however, information is publicly acquired by a 'broker' the position is different. There is no professional confidentiality to invoke to keep the informant safe, and obviously the newspaper knows that the information 'on sale' is of 'questionable origin'. In such a case,

---

[18] The messages related to the topic '*Re: Los Angeles Times article on Helsingius and anon.penet.fi*' are still available at: http://cypherpunks.venona.com/date/1996/09/msg00200.html (visited 28 December 2018).

[19] ibid.

[20] Stefania Maurizi, 'WikiLeaks rivela l'ultimo allarme per la diga di Mosul', *La Repubblica* online edition, 21 December 2018: https://www.repubblica.it/esteri/2018/12/21/news/wikileaks_allarme_diga_mosul_ambasciate-214804434/ (visited 23 December 2018).

the broker is incentivised to strengthen its anonymity-securing infrastructure to render the life of its 'contributors' easier, therefore gathering more and more information to be made (temporarily) available in an exclusive form to its various clients.

The clients – in this case, the newspapers – know that compensating the broker will ensure that it continues to provide them additional material. Who would dare describe this as receiving stolen property, warranting criminal prosecution?

After more than 29 years, Esther Dyson's warning about being accountable for what one publishes online still resonates: It is not a question of privacy. It is important to prevent the right to privacy collapsing into the right to secrecy or – as the GDPR seems to imply – into the right to pseudonymity.

III. Anonymous Remailers

Among the most effective anonymous remailer systems currently available are the German Tutanota and the Dutch StartMail, whose CEO has asserted, 'As early as 2005 we recognized privacy as a fundamental human right.'[21] But he continues by reiterating Schneier's mantra: 'Privacy and security must go hand in hand. There can be no privacy without security.'[22]

The reality, of course, is that the likes of StartMail offer merely the factual state or condition of security, secrecy, or anonymity rather than privacy as a legal right.

A more extreme approach is adopted by Tutanota.com, which, committing the same error, summarises its services as follows: 'Tutanota does not track its users or log IP addresses because we believe that everybody has a right to communicate anonymously with each other.'[23] Furthermore, while StartMail provides its users with relative anonymity in return for payment (by sharing information between itself and the payment processor) Tutanota allows donations and payments by way of cryptocurrencies such as Bitcoin, Ether and Monero (the latter promising actual untraceability.)

Both companies' terms and conditions clearly state that they neither condone nor support unlawful conduct, but this is wishful thinking, because as soon as you have an account that – from payment to use – is fully untraceable there is no actual way to distinguish (at least pre-emptively) an unlawful misuse from a legitimate use.

From the data protection perspective, these services appear, especially when viewed through the distorted lens of the right to privacy, to be in almost perfect compliance with the GDPR's prescriptions. This is indeed the case from the user's

---

[21] Robert Beens, *Privacy. It's not just our policy. It's our mission* https://www.startmail.com/en/privacy/ (visited 28 December 2018).
[22] ibid.
[23] https://tutanota.com/blog/posts/anonymous-email/ (visited 28 December 2018).

point of view. But from the perspective of the victim of a scam, a threat or a defamatory publication, the situation is rather different.

The duty of fairness in the processing of personal data imposed by the GDPR must be globally assessed to take into account the protection of the victim. In other words, a fully anonymous system that – as a matter of fact – allows an untraceable entity to process third party's personal data without being accountable would infringe the duty of fairness and, thus, would be unlawful.

While this (paradoxical) argument is compelling in relation to the protection of personal data, it does not operate very smoothly when applied to the right to control personal information.

And this problem is a consequence of the incoherence of the concept of privacy which, as argued throughout this work, comprises two elements: first, the right of an individual to choose what personal information should be shared, and, secondly, the right of the individual to maintain control over the personal information shared. StartMail, Tutanota and similar services are useful tools, but they merely facilitate the actual exercise of this right of the individual over personal information and, as such, cannot be considered per se illegal.

Accepting this approach illuminates the crucial point that in order successfully to protect the right to privacy, 'privacy' must be severed from its ties with both factual conditions (secrecy, anonymity) and other rights, interests, and values provisions (free speech, confidentiality of communication, regulation of search and seizure and so on). This muddle entangles privacy in a Gordian Knot. And, as a side effect, it confirms that the right to privacy is not – and cannot be conceived as – a shield from wrongdoing, as almost every politician of democratic persuasion routinely claims.

From this perspective, the debate 'anonymity versus full identifiability' that from time to time sparks political discourse loses its privacy-centric character and displays its true colours: a means by which to restrict free speech. An example of this tendency is the draft Bill recently presented by the Italian Senator, Nazario Pagano.[24] A clause in the Bill provides for the requirement that a permanent caching service provider must request the user for a state-issued ID during the registration phase. This proposal deftly distances itself from any privacy-related issues, as the question of anonymity is dealt with in relation to freedom of speech rather than privacy. Consequently, the Bill maintains the need for an official ID as a prerequisite to support investigations by law enforcement authorities 'just in case'. It therefore affirms that there is no threat whatsoever to free speech and 'protects' the victims of criminal behaviour.

---

[24] Disegno di legge 895 *Modifica al decreto legislativo 9 aprile 2003, n. 70, recante attuazione della direttiva 2000/31/CE relativa a taluni aspetti giuridici dei servizi della società dell'informazione nel mercato interno, con particolare riferimento al commercio elettronico, in materia di identificazione dei destinatari dei servizi*: http://www.senato.it/service/PDF/PDFServer/BGT/01082988.pdf (visited 28 December 2018).

It may be thought that the victims this Bill has at its heart are those who suffer scams, breaches of privacy, or violence. But the official report that encapsulates the Bill's contents reveals that the criminal offences taken as paradigmatic examples are confined to defamation and generic 'threats'.[25] And while the Bill was subsequently extended to increase the list of criminal offences that its proponent claims to be concerned about, the focus remains on social network trolls and those who despise politicians![26]

It is difficult to avoid the conclusion that this proposed legislation is designed to act as a deterrent against the voices of users of social networking platforms. In other words, its purpose appears to be curtailing the freedom to criticise the powers-that-be by preventing strong opinions, rather than penalising those who abuse freedom of speech.

A similar instance of the mistaken relationship between privacy and secrecy comes from Australia, where on 6 December 2018 its Parliament passed the Telecommunications and Other Legislation Amendment (Assistance and Access) Act 2018.[27] According to the official summary, this law amends other legislation currently in force

> [T]o establish frameworks for voluntary and mandatory industry assistance to law enforcement and intelligence agencies in relation to encryption technologies via the issuing of technical assistance requests, technical assistance notices and technical capability notices.

In plain English, this is a measure by which to compel 'industry' (ie, microprocessor and other components' manufacturers as well as software developers and telecom/internet operators) to assist in cracking, or to crack on the state's behalf, users' communications.

Thus, in a pincer movement, while the Italian Bill attacks the secrecy of the unaccountable, the Australian law crushes the secrecy of the communications of identified persons. Both the individual and his or her communications are strangled in a lethal bear-hold. And both the Italian Bill and the new Australian statute are (unbeknown to each other) interconnected by a classic, privacy-related conundrum: being unaccountable for one's own action is the need that fuels both secrecy and anonymity. Sometimes being anonymous and 'enjoying' a state of secrecy is a legitimate goal, where, for instance political activists require covertness or where investigative journalists operate to expose misconduct.[28]

---

[25] *Relazione al Disegno di Legge 895*, p 2: http://www.senato.it/service/PDF/PDFServer/BGT/01082988.pdf (visited 28 December 2018).

[26] *RAI Parlamento*, 'Web. Contro le insidie della rete', *Sette Giorni*, 1 December 2018 available at: http://www.rai.it/dl/RaiTV/programmi/media/ContentItem-ed007c74-8385-4c7c-9cc7-07725014adb8.html#p=.

[27] Australian Parliament, *Telecommunications and Other Legislation Amendment (Assistance and Access) Bill 2018* https://www.aph.gov.au/Parliamentary_Business/Bills_Legislation/Bills_Search_Results/Result?bId=r6195 (visited 28 December 2018).

[28] See generally, Sissela Bok, *Secrets: On the Ethics of Concealment and Revelation* (New York: Vintage Books, 1998).

Where (and how) do we draw a line between the legitimate exercise of the right to privacy and the need to uncover wrongdoing?

IV. Cryptocurrencies

One answer may be found in the debate surrounding cryptocurrencies. The discussion above referred to the (almost) anonymity available online along with the embedding of an anonymity-by-design technology. User anonymity is pursued by accepting (quasi)anonymous payment systems and cryptocurrencies, thus defeating – or at least, weakening – the 'follow the money' investigation technique.

This is hardly novel. Long before the emergence of digital currencies, traditional cash-based transactions were known as a means by which to launder money, evade tax, and other nefarious conduct. They were therefore subjected to increasingly rigorous regulation which led to greater use of electronically traceable transactions. In this regard, Bitcoin and its siblings do not pose 'new legal challenges', but as in other cases, the legal assessment of cryptocurrency is influenced by a cultural prejudice that privileges technology over legal analysis. But should it?

Letters of exchange date back to the twelfth century and *Hawala* – the Arab equivalent – even to the eighth century. Both were systems that performed a function entirely similar to that performed by cryptocurrency: to transfer value without necessarily moving money. And when securities, derivatives and other objects of financial engineering took on an autonomous value, freed from any connection with reserves or currencies, it was evident that the Emperor was naked and legal currency, dead. Or, better still, artificially kept alive in a system that, thanks to the dematerialisation of information and value, no longer needs physical tinsel to define and move wealth. The only genuine problem raised by cryptocurrencies, then, is not juridical but political, and comprises the loss of control by the state over value and wealth; that is, in short, the loss of an instrument of social control.[29]

From this perspective, even if cryptocurrencies provide absolute anonymity – a claim that, at least in regard to Bitcoin, has not been demonstrated so far[30] – the matter would be related to the technical resources necessary under a specific legal framework to identify people engaged in a transaction rather than to the

---

[29] Andrea Monti, 'A contribution to the Analysis of the Legal Status of Cryptocurrencies' *Ragion Pratica Rivista semestrale* 2/2018, p 378, doi: 10.1415/91544. English translation by Andrea Monti.

[30] See Stefano Zanero, M Spagnuolo and F Maggi, 'Bitiodine: Extracting Intelligence from the Bitcoin Network' in N Christin and R Safavi-Naini (eds), *Financial Cryptography and Data Security* (International Conference on Financial Cryptography and Data Security) (Berlin: Springer, 2014) 457–68. The complete history of all transactions ever performed, called 'blockchain', is public and replicated on each node. The data it contains is difficult to analyse manually, but can yield a significant amount of relevant information. This paper 'present[s] a modular framework, BitIodine... [that] label[s] users automatically or semi-automatically with information on who they are and what they do' which is automatically 'scraped' from openly available information sources.

supposed innate *contra legem* nature of cryptocurrencies or a potential infringement of the right to privacy.

But to adhere to the traditional, 'privacy-as-none-of-your-business' approach would render this conclusion very hard to sustain. Giving (crypto)currency to support political activists, accepting it as a payment from a blacklisted country for having infringed the embargo on certain goods, or using it to purchase recreational drugs are different forms of activities with different legal characteristics, and a case-by-case analysis to determine whether (the mistaken, secrecy-oriented notion of) the right to privacy is involved would be pointless. It would destroy the essential nature of this fundamental right.

V. Sexual Preference

Disentangling the intersection between privacy and other values may prove to be a valuable means by which to expound a viable, legal definition of the right to privacy. This is especially evident where the right to privacy is deployed as a means to protect minority rights, as has occurred in the case of homosexual relationships.[31]

Several jurisdictions have addressed this matter, and assumed, as the Delhi High Court did, in a case involving gay rights, that

> The sphere of privacy allows persons to develop human relations without interference from the outside community or from the State. The exercise of autonomy enables an individual to attain fulfilment, grow in self-esteem, build relationships of his or her choice and fulfil all legitimate goals that he or she may set.[32]

The Indian Supreme Court, in what has been called[33] a 'landmark ruling',[34] recently upheld this interpretation while still failing to provide a distinctive, lucid definition of privacy. On the contrary, the Indian decision makes – and perpetuates – the typical error of mixing different rights and different levels of protection. Referring to the rights of homosexuals, the Court rightly asserts the principle that:

> Yet in a democratic Constitution founded on the rule of law, their rights are as sacred as those conferred on other citizens to protect their freedoms and liberties. Sexual orientation is an essential attribute of privacy. Discrimination against an individual on the basis of sexual orientation is deeply offensive to the dignity and self-worth of the individual. Equality demands that the sexual orientation of each individual in society must

---

[31] See the discussion of the leading United States Supreme Court decisions in Chapter 1.

[32] *Naz Foundation v Government of NCT of Delhi*, 9 July 2009 (2010) *Crim LJ* 94 (Del), 110 at [48].

[33] Geeta Pandey, 'Indian Supreme Court in Landmark Ruling on Privacy', *BBC News* online, 24 August 2017: https://www.bbc.com/news/world-asia-india-41033954 (visited 28 December 2018).

[34] *Justice KS Puttaswamy (Rtd) and another v Union of India and others*, 24 August 2017: https://www.sci.gov.in/supremecourt/2012/35071/35071_2012_Judgement_24-Aug-2017.pdf.

be protected on an even platform. The right to privacy and the protection of sexual orientation lie at the core of the fundamental rights guaranteed by Articles 14, 15 and 21 of the Constitution.[35]

But is privacy the appropriate legal tool to protect a minority's rights?

Affirming that (the right to) dignity is protected by (the right to) secrecy enhances, but does not eliminate discrimination against members of a minority. Where legal protection collapses into privacy-as-secrecy, what is actually achieved is a hypocritical approach of the outmoded 'don't ask, don't tell' kind.

In contrast, by acknowledging human beings for their human nature – rather than importing other factors – we recognise and respect their essential dignity, without drawing an arbitrary distinction between the private and the public realm.

VI. Scientific Positivism

The relevance of the right to dignity over (a muddled notion of) privacy is more apparent when the question of gay rights – and generally those of minorities – is dealt with by way of technology or 'scientifically'.

All forms of discrimination involve the denial of human beings of their 'human' condition, and assigning them a 'different' category, whether this be ethnic, religious, or physical/biological. This process is well explained by Lt Col Dave Grossman in his classic essay on the social cost of learning to kill:

> Unlike the victims of aerial bombing, the victims of these [concentration] camps had to look their sadistic killers in the face and know that another human being denied their humanity and hated them enough to personally slaughter them, their families, and their race as though they were nothing more than animals.[36]

Discrimination against the 'other' is, of course, irrational, but what if these specious grounds were based on science and technology? Such ideas are not new; in the nineteenth century positivists like Cesare Lombroso sought a 'scientific' basis on which to classify human beings objectively into different categories of criminals. And later the early findings of pre-genetics biology produced the multiple racial theories that fuelled Nazi ideology.

Recent studies[37] hint at a possible biological root of androphilia,[38] but a definitive conclusion is far from being reached, and the connection with specific

---

[35] ibid, at [126].

[36] Dave Grossman, *On Killing: The Psychological Cost of Learning to Kill in War and Society* (New York: Open Road Media, 2014) 78.

[37] Debra Soh, 'Cross-Cultural Evidence for the Genetics of Homosexuality', *Scientific American*, online edition, 25 April 2017: https://www.scientificamerican.com/article/cross-cultural-evidence-for-the-genetics-of-homosexuality/ (visited 29 December 2017.)

[38] Sexual attraction of biological males to men or masculinity.

chromosomes is still merely speculative.[39] But even if such a connection could be discovered, it would have no impact in regard to the right to privacy. A democratic society is committed to treating all individuals equally, regardless of their sexual proclivities or gender.

Consequently, by conceiving 'privacy' as the right to live in seclusion and anonymity, and thereby according minorities a personal status (be it biological, cultural, or whatever) fails to protect them. It is, on the contrary, the right of members of a minority to assert their identity publicly. The right to privacy, in other words, is not an effective protection because it is based on keeping the world out of an individual's existence; the law ought instead to create an environment in which members of a minority are able to live openly in the world.

It is not only (bad or misinterpreted) science that has driven discriminatory ideologies. Military technology has also played its part. Dehumanisation may be achieved even without invoking racial or genetic differences; all that is required is space and distance. The transformation of armed conflict from the close-quarter, bloody and personal into distant and impersonal using the remote killing machines of artillery and carpet bombing, and lately video game-like drone raids has abetted the process of dehumanisation:

> Social distance is generally fading as a form of killing enabling in Western war. But even as it disappears in this more egalitarian age, it is being replaced by a new, technologically based form of psychological distance. During the Gulf War this was referred to as 'Nintendo warfare,' which evolved into 'video game combat' in Iraq and Afghanistan ... Night-vision devices provide a superb form of psychological distance by converting the target into an inhuman green blob.[40]

This grisly development occurs not only through a set of strong cultural/social or political beliefs, but technology is also implicated. In fact, its contribution is considerably more perilous than the racial superiority claims of 'science' because it simply skips these 'technicalities' by focusing on the external perception, with no apparent ethical commitment.

The judicial enforcement of (a variant of) the Implicit Association Test (IAT) is a striking example of the (tragic) mistakes that can occur by stretching the operational limit of empirical social analysis tools to convert their findings from a trend indicator into a veracity device. This anonymous, survey-based test measures 'attitudes and beliefs that people may be unwilling or unable to report. The IAT may be especially interesting if it shows that you have an implicit attitude that you did not know about'.[41]

---

[39] Alan Sanders et al, 'Genome-Wide Association Study of Male Sexual Orientation', *Scientific Reports*, 7 December 2017 (Nature Publishing Group): https://www.nature.com/articles/s41598-017-15736-4 (visited 28 December 2018).

[40] Dave Grossman, *On Killing*, n 36 above, 169–70.

[41] Harvard University Project Implicit 'About the *IAT*': https://implicit.harvard.edu/implicit/education.html (visited 28 December 2018).

Harvard University's Project Implicit[42] runs an online version of the IAT that collects the participant's personal information (age, profession, political orientation, sex assigned at birth, current sex, country of origin, country of residence, etc) on an opt-in basis. Once the preliminary phase is completed, the platform guides the individual through a five-stage interactive procedure in which answers are provided by pressing the 'E' and 'I' keys on the keyboard in relation to the association between a displayed image and a previously defined category (ie, white people, black people, harmless object, weapons). The result is a chart that is supposed to show the participant's attitudes toward the topics. Another survey checks whether the results actually match the participant's attitude.

The IAT, far from being a genuinely 'scientific'[43] test, has provided results in general terms and has been studied as a tool to address the problem of implicit bias in (US) jury selection[44] but its application, or more precisely, the application of its variant, on an individual scale failed to work as advertised.

As argued throughout this book, there is a red line that connects every attempt to exploit personal information for diverse motives: the prediction of the behaviour of a single individual. Be it for commercial purposes, obtaining compliance, or garnering political support, the objective is the same: a shift from a statistical model describing 'trends' to casting a spell in order to obtain a yes/no response from an individual.

The IAT is by no means alien to this logic, and soon a version of this test is to be enforced on a limited scale for legal purposes. This is the autobiographical Implicit Association Test (aIAT), 'a novel application of the implicit association concept for detecting life events. It has been used to reveal concealed knowledge in clinical and forensic settings, including detecting drug use.'[45] The main difference between IAT and aIAT is that the latter works on the participant's memory and recollection of facts rather than on attitudes toward abstract categories and individual beliefs not related to specific and potentially self-indicting circumstances.

Unquestionably, and in theory, the aIAT is of considerable interest to the legal community, but it is still in a very early stage of independent assessment and as such should not be used in court. Owing to the attractiveness of having a fast, portable, and economical tool to identify 'guilty' in a large unknown population, it is expected that the response-time-based 'lie-detectors' will continue to attract

---

[42] Project Implicit: http://www.projectimplicit.net/index.html (visited 28 December 2018).

[43] Graham Healy et al, 'Neural Patterns of the Implicit Association Test', *Frontiers in Human Neuroscience*, 24 November 2015, 9:605.

[44] Mark W Bennett, 'Unraveling the Gordian Knot of Implicit Bias in Jury Selection: The Problems of Judge-Dominated Voir Dire, the Failed Promise of *Batson*, and Proposed Solutions' (2010) 149 *Harvard Law & Policy Review* 1207. https://www.americanbar.org/content/dam/aba/administrative/labor_law/meetings/2011/eeo/057.authcheckdam.pdf (visited 28 December 2018).

[45] Elisabeth Julie Vargo and Andrea Petróczi, 'Detecting Cocaine Use? The Autobiographical Implicit Association Test (aIAT) Produces False Positives in a Real-world Setting' (2013) 8 *Substance Abuse Treatment, Prevention, and Policy*, doi:10.1186/1747-597X-8-22.

attention of researchers and practitioners alike. More research into the aIAT's functioning is strongly advised before further forensic use of the instrument, to ensure that vicarious experiences and other mental associations do not confound results.[46]

Notwithstanding the vagueness of the aIAT results in relation to an individual, there has been at least one judicial application of this method in a legal battle between the Corte di cassazione (the Italian Supreme Court) and two courts of appeal which had rejected the aIAT from the realm of 'scientific evidence'.[47]

In 2012 the Court of Appeal of Catanzaro was asked the re-hear a criminal case on the basis of alleged 'new scientific evidence': the aIAT. The defendant had been charged with having acted in concert with others to commit murder. According to the defendant, the aIAT could prove that his memory did not contain any recollection of the murder, and he should therefore be acquitted. The Court of Catanzaro rejected his appeal, holding that there were no sources to assess either the novelty or the scientific validity of aIAT as evidence.

The defendant appealed to the Corte di cassazione that, incredibly, overruled[48] the lower court's judgment. In but a few lines, the Supreme Court stated that it was a duty of the Court of Appeal to assess the validity of the aIAT instead of putting the burden of proving it on the defence-appointed expert, and sent the case to a different Court of Appeal (the Court of Salerno) to issue another verdict.

On 16 December 2016 the Salerno court, addressing the point raised by the Supreme Court, again denied the appellant a retrial, finding that:

> the IAT test, used in social psychology to evaluate stereotypes, prejudices, implicit attitudes towards consumer products or political candidates, is something profoundly different from the a-IAT that seeks the amnestic trace of an event; that the autobiographical memory is a very complex concept with which the auto-narrative that the subject makes of a certain event interacts (and the appellant had, for some time, structured in his personal narrative, a story that excluded the event); that there was no validation of the method proposed in the scientific literature.[49]

This case raises a number of questions, but the principal one is the role of pseudoscience, based on the accumulation of anonymous personal information, in influencing our beliefs and promoting discrimination without infringing any right to privacy. IAT, aIAT and its siblings can be administered in such a way as to respect the personal information of respondents, but this does not mean that they will not affect other individual rights that are endangered by these forms of neo-positivism.

---

[46] Elisabeth Julie Vargo, Andrea Petróczi, ibid.

[47] The detailed account of this case is documented in Giuseppe Gennari, 'La macchina della verità si è fermata a Salerno … fortunatamente' (2018) 12 *Diritto Penale Contemporaneo*.

[48] Corte di Cassazione, Fifth Criminal Branch, Decision n. 14255 issued on 2 January 2013, available at: https://www.penalecontemporaneo.it/upload/2703-cass-14255-2013.pdf (visited 28 December 2018.)

[49] Giuseppe Gennari, 'La macchina della verità si è fermata a Salerno', n 47 above, 13.

And their effects on the protection of personal information are clear. When these 'mind-miners' dig deeper into a human brain, there will be fewer opportunities to protect our inner self by controlling what information we want to share, and what is intended for our eyes only. But this concern is one principally of freedom rather than privacy. In fact, the current exploitation of behavioural analysis methods and of IAT or IAT-like tools has the capacity to produce results that have more far reaching consequences than have been imagined.

As in the case of the impact of a national DNA database on government political strategies (discussed in Chapter three), the aggregation of (anonymous) personal information related to the attitudes of individuals can negatively affect individual freedom both globally and locally. One need only take one of the *Project Implicit* surveys to question whether it is actually reasonable – and to what extent – to trust its results. Moreover, these results are available to the general public as research materials, consulting services to detect implicit bias in the workplace, and so on.[50]

It is not within the scope of this book to challenge any specific research project or business model, but it is clearly evident that, especially when dealing with individuals and individuals' right, the *in vivo* exploitation of methods to analyse their inner selves should meet a very high standard of scientific review and acceptance.

This is not the place to examine the question of what constitutes legitimate scientific enquiry,[51] but it is certainly the case that in some fields – for instance, medical research – more than in others there is likely to be greater social acceptance of the quid pro quo: personal information in exchange for the possibility of new cures or treatments for diseases.

Traditionally, medical research is based on the collection of a wide variety of information, ranging from vital parameters to living habits. Where a disease under investigation is especially intractable, no hypothesis can be excluded and every piece of information might be useful:

> Science begins with counting. To understand a phenomenon, a scientist must first describe it; to describe it objectively, he must first measure it. If cancer medicine was to be transformed into a rigorous science, then cancer would need to be counted somehow – measured in some reliable, reproducible way.[52]

In other words, seeking to combat a disease is a no-holds-barred struggle; individual rights may be sacrificed on the altar of medical advances. Nevertheless, this

---

[50] https://www.projectimplicit.net/services.html (visited 28 December 2018.)

[51] Sociologists, psychologists, economists and legal scholars – just to name a few – like to regard themselves as 'scientists', but, as a general proposition, they are not, because their discipline does not meet the requirements of a genuine science. This is not to say their work lacks rigour and logic, and operates within a certain canon, but a true science is something else. From an epistemological perspective, of course, it is not easy to discern what constitutes 'science', and the philosophical debate has moved on beyond Popper's doctrine of falsifiability. See, for example, the analysis of the concept of 'scientific *phrónesis*' by Giovanni Boniolo, *Metodo e rappresentazioni del mondo: per un'altra filosofia della scienza* (Milan, Bruno Mondadori, 1999) 54.

[52] Siddhartha Mukherjee, *The Emperor of All Maladies* (New York: Harper Collins, 2011) 19.

ought not to justify extreme measures such as, for example, using human beings as guinea pigs against their will or compelling individuals to participate in clinical trials. But the tendency to treat 'privacy' as an absolute is equally undesirable. This attitude is often to be observed in certain European data protection authorities when considering medical or genetic research.[53]

The statement of the Italian Data Protection Commissioner (quoted verbatim in note 53 below), in addition to being wrong, contradicts the declaration of principle in the GDPR:

> The processing of personal data should be designed to serve mankind. The right to the protection of personal data is not an absolute right; it must be considered in relation to its function in society and be balanced against other fundamental rights, in accordance with the principle of proportionality.

Furthermore, there is no legal ground for a Data Protection Authority to assert its regulatory power directly over a bio-sample. A bio-sample is not 'personal information' but merely a very large chemical compound from which a series of data can be obtained. Only when the data are matched with the knowledge of the researcher does it become 'information'. And only when this information is associated with a specific identity, does it become 'personal data' and thus relevant to the GDPR.

Finally, by interpreting the data protection regulations so that they limit both scientific research and clinical trials – which are, in any event, regulated by international conventions, EU regulations, and European guidelines – is to impose unnecessary burdens on activities whose only aim is to save lives or allow people to die with dignity.

Requiring written consent to be obtained for almost everything (relatives included, in case of inherited diseases) is inviting bureaucracy and expense merely to prevent a possible misuse of personal information that might not even occur. And it undermines medical research.

---

[53] For instance, in an interview in *La Stampa* on 31 October 2017, the Italian Data Protection Commissioner stated: 'If it is true that a profit can be gained from the research on human biological material, it is true – too – that there is no such thing as biobank ownership, but only the right to research the available samples.' But actually, at least under Italian law, this is not true because human tissues, once taken, become *res nullius* and therefore can be owned by a research facility. There is no specific case law in Italy but, as Jennifer Wagner points out, the principle that tissue removed from patients no longer belongs to them has long been the law in the United States. Jennifer K Wagner, 'Property Rights and the Human Body', *Privacy Report*, 11 June 2014. https://theprivacyreport.com/2014/06/11/property-rights-and-the-human-body/. See *Moore v Regents of the University of California*, 51 Cal 3d 120, 271 Cal Rptr 146; 793 P 2d 479 (Cal, 1990) https://scocal.stanford.edu/opinion/moore-v-regents-university-california-31115 (visited 30 December 2018); *Washington University v Catalona*: http://media.ca8.uscourts.gov/opndir/07/06/062286P.pdf (visited 30 December 2018). It has been similarly decided in *Piljak Estate v Abraham* 2014 ONSC 2893, in Canada: see Richard Warnica, 'Human Tissue Removed for Medical Tests is "Personal Property" of Institution, not Person it came From: Ruling', *National Post* online edition, 5 June 2014: https://nationalpost.com/news/canada/human-tissue-removed-for-medical-tests-is-personal-property-of-institution-not-person-it-came-from-ruling (visited 30 December 2018).

In fact, the provisions of the GDPR point to a rather different approach; recital 2 declares:

> This Regulation is intended to contribute to the accomplishment of an area of freedom, security and justice and of an economic union, to economic and social progress, to the strengthening and the convergence of the economies within the internal market, and to the *well-being of natural persons* (emphasis added).

VII. Genetic Research

This is really an umbrella definition that covers a range of different activities, from genetic sequencing to biobanks management to bioengineering. Many procedures do not fit into this description. Therefore, when considering the GDPR and genetic research, one needs first to examine the objectives and methodology of the proposed research project. For example, a recent research paper published in *Nature*, 'Correction of a Pathogenic Gene Mutation in Human Embryos'[54] explores the hypothesis that some genetic mutations might be corrected in human gametes or early embryos by way of the CRISPR-Cas9 technique. In fact, the paper has no connection with the GDPR, since its authors are from South Korea, China, and the United States. Nevertheless – precisely for this reason – it is instructive to examine it from a GDPR perspective.

The subject of the research was the MYBPC3 gene mutation related to Hypertrophic Cardiomyopathy or HCM, a heart-related genetic disease, investigated because of its significant frequency among humans. The research involved the processing of ethnicity and/or identified patient-related data, and since there is considerable interest in preventing second-generation transmission, this might require the processing of patients' ancestors and living descendants. Furthermore, the genetic information of a set of 19 embryos was included as a control group. Finally, the personal data of the donors were used without anonymisation, as their identity could be deduced by the informed consent of the participants.[55]

Recruiting of patients involved another area of genetic/health-related personal data:

> Healthy gamete donors were recruited locally, via print and web-based advertising. Homozygous and heterozygous adult patients with known heritable MYBPC3 mutations were sought; however, only three adult heterozygous patients were identified by

---

[54] Shoukhrat Malipov, et al, 'Correction of a Pathogenic Gene Mutation in Human Embryos', *Nature* online edition: http://www.nature.com/nature/journal/v548/n7668/full/nature23305.html (visited 30 December 2018),

[55] The Informed Consent template used in the participant recruiting phase shows that the researchers were able to trace the donors' identity in every phase of their activity; this is evident from the possibility, given to the donors, to be informed of important health-related issues that might come to light as a 'collateral effect' of the research.

OHSU Knight Cardiovascular Institute physicians and referred to the research team, one of whom agreed to participate in the study.[56]

To summarise, the personal information-gathering process employed was as follows. First, a group of scientists belonging to different institutions located in different parts of the world defined the goal of the research and its methodology, including, for instance, the use of bio-samples, cellular lines and so on. Secondly, the researchers sought healthy individuals, and requested a hospital to select patients who might be interested in the project. The data of both the patients and the healthy individuals were then processed throughout the whole study so that each individual's identity was known to the researchers. Thirdly, while informed consent was obtained from those who agreed to participate into the study, there is no information about how the pre-screening phase was conducted by the hospital that selected the prospective patients. Fourthly, specific, identified individuals were targeted by the researchers who were aware that the patients' ancestors and descendants might also be suffering from the disease, but the paper contains no information about how the researchers discovered the identity of the patients' relatives. Finally, part of the research was based on statistical information involving ethnic origins.

Looking at the study from an EU data protection standpoint reveals a number of grey areas in the processing of personal information, mainly in the way in which information and consent were obtained. The ideal model by which to handle genetic/health-related personal information according to EU legislation is to assess, as a primary step, which of the collected data fall within the GDPR definition of personal information (information that identifies a natural person or renders him or her identifiable).

The GDPR would treat the ethnicity of the disease-affected individuals as merely statistical information, while the selected (and rejected) patients, and their relatives, as well as the healthy individuals clearly fall into the category of data subjects. A more complex question is whether the information extracted from DNA that is 'cut' by the CRISPR-Cas9 method constitutes 'personal information' as defined. There is a point where information related to an individual loses its personal quality and becomes 'neutral'; it is thus beyond the reach of the GDPR. It would be hard to argue that knowledge of the chemical elements of which we are made is personal information processing.

A less extreme example is the portion of DNA to be edited to remove a defective part. This plainly belongs to a specific human being, but the information it provides loses its 'identifying power' precisely because the results of the editing process can be extended to whomever shares the same pathological condition and are no longer unequivocally connected to a single, specific person. In other words, this is a variation of the classical Sorites Paradox that, in its legal form,

---

[56] Shoukhrat Malipov, et al, n 54 above.

becomes: is it possible that at a certain point, after tearing apart information related to an individual, this information, while still connected to him or her, loses its quality of being personal information?

The second matter to evaluate is which of the collected data fall within the scope of the GDPR (protection of personal information to be processed by way of a filing system). Here matters become complicated. As far as can be determined by scrutinising the paper, while the control group information has somehow been organised into a *structure*, it should be processed according to the GDPR, at least in regard to the accidental discovery of health problems since each research-participant patient's data were processed individually. This means that while such information is personal, it might not be subject to the GDPR because of the lack of a filing system as part of the processing.

Thirdly, the purpose of the processing must be defined. As clearly stated by the researchers, the goal of the research is to look for a method by which to use CRISPR-Cas9 to 'delete' a specific mutation. This suggests that the processing of genetic information is a means to an end, and an end in itself. In other words, the researchers' expected outcome is an answer to a general question and not a result tailored to the patient's needs/conditions. This is a fine distinction; there is a difference between the processing of personal information as the purpose of the processing, on the one hand, and the processing of personal information as a way to manipulate chemical, person-unrelated portions of a genetic compound.

Scientific and, in particular, genetic research is supported by a strong justification, and its methodology makes it difficult to obtain the consent to personal information processing for every collateral branch of investigation that might stem from the main research tree.

A balanced approach between the right of the data subject and the 'greater good' pursued by the scientist is called for. It should take into account, as the GDPR itself provides, the risks to the individual's dignity and other fundamental rights, in order not unreasonably to restrict or discourage vital scientific advances, especially in preventing and treating disease.

While it does not pose a high risk, the processing of patients' clinical information during the selection phase, some personal and control group information, (as soon as it is done by way of a filing system) should be conducted under the aegis of a hospital's ethics committee. This requires properly informing both the patients and the members of the control group and obtaining informed consent, as stated in the GDPR's recital 33.

It is often not possible completely to identify the purpose of personal data processing for scientific research at the time of data collection. Therefore, data subjects should be permitted to give their consent to certain areas of scientific research when it is in keeping with recognised ethical standards. Data subjects should have the opportunity to provide their informed consent only to certain areas of research or parts of research projects, to the extent allowed by the intended purpose.

Of course, if the process is fully anonymised, for instance by having the hospital retain the patient/volunteer identity separate from the rest of the medical record, and having a third party collect and organise the information, the research would not be subject to the GDPR because there is no way in which the researchers could trace the participants' identities. Should this anonymisation process become standard practice, it would represent an acceptable balancing between the rights of data subjects and the needs of science.

A final matter is that of DNA manipulation. While my DNA clearly belongs to me, the object of data processing is related to the behaviour of the chemical compound, not me! Again, a fair balance needs to be struck between individual rights and public needs. Where this is achieved, there is room to conclude that the GDPR should not apply. As complex and difficult as the practical enforcement of the GDPR is in such circumstances, a practical and prudent interpretation of the provisions would facilitate this research within the EU with a higher degree of confidence that such studies are wholly compliant with the law.

Unfortunately, the manner in which data protection regulation is widely interpreted is based on a pre-emptive rather than on ex post facto control. This translates into a huge waste of resources to prevent something that might never occur, without any benefit to the affected data subject and patients in the community at large.

A more sensible approach – entirely consistent with the GDPR – would allow the easing of the pre-emptive burden on researchers' shoulders while enforcing strict controls over actual cases, whether or not the processing of personal data is carried out safely.

In conclusion it should be noted that medical information is not ipso facto 'personal information' as understood in this book. The positive results of a routine check-up which reveal the identity of the patient is clearly 'personal data' as defined by the GDPR. The disclosure of this information is unlikely to occasion anxiety on the part of the patient. On the contrary, if the same check-up discloses evidence of a pathological condition, the patient is fully entitled to exercise control over its exposure, even if it is outside the purview of the GDPR (because, for instance, it is neither intended to be automatically processed nor used by means of a filing system). In this case the right to privacy as control over personal information acts in a complementary way to the GDPR, covering the space left unattended by the EU regulation.

Furthermore, there is an important distinction between information as fact (my blood pressure), information as conjecture (there is a 70 per cent probability that I may develop Alzheimer's disease), information as deduction (the analysis of all my physiological parameters points to my having a certain pathological condition) and, information that is 'personal' (I do not wish my medical condition to be known by others).

Does a researcher have the right to access – or manipulate – such information? Or, from a different perspective, do those affected by a certain illness have the right that others be compelled to allow their personal information to be processed to increase the hope of finding a cure? Such questions cannot be answered in legal terms as the answers require a prior ethical and political debate involving the balancing of protection of the individual and scientific progress.

An unfortunate paradox is that however this conflict is resolved, a freedom is sacrificed: the freedom of individuals over their lives or the freedom of individuals to explore the mysteries of the universe.

VIII. Copyright

The taxonomy of rights related to bio-information and fundamental rights would be incomplete without a brief reference to the problems created by the expansion of the reach of this aspect of intellectual property.

For centuries, copyright has protected artists, writers, and musicians. The adoption of EU Directive 518/92, however, changed forever the legal landscape of creative works by acknowledging that software and, later, the structuring of databases are to be considered as creative acts and therefore to be protected by the right of their 'author'. It is probable that no member of the EU Parliament was aware that the with the enactment of this directive the European Union would open a Pandora's Box, allowing the enforcement of copyright far more comprehensive than was originally believed, and extending as far as bio-information.

In 1992, using copyright as a way to secure some sort of intellectual property protection over bio-information was not actually something new. A few years earlier, Walter Gilbert, one of the pioneers of research in this field, told the *Washington Post*:

> I don't think the genome is patentable. What interests us is to impose copyright on the sequences. This means that if someone wants to read the code, they will have to pay for the right to access it. Our aim is to make information available to everyone. As long as they pay a price.[57]

It might have been thought that that such a development would never take place, at least in Europe, given that the GDPR, which qualifies genetic data as 'particular' is a first defence against this attempt at 'misappropriation'. Besides, genetic sequences as such possess no creative character and cannot, therefore, be protected by copyright. Nevertheless, the GDPR has no jurisdiction over genetic sequences and bio-information, because in many cases, especially where the research is not dependent on the association between a genetic sample and the donor, the information is essentially anonymous. As such it is easier to process.

Moreover, the sequences as such cannot really be considered as the outcome of an 'act of creativity'. Certainly the protection earmarked to databases by the

---

[57] Larry Thompson, 'Genes, Politics and Money: Biologists' Most Ambitious Project Will Cost a Fortune, But Its Value Could Be Beyond Measure', *The Washington Post*, 24 February 1987.

EU Directive allows creators of a genetic database to exclude whoever they wish from accessing the information and criminalises extracting the contents of the database without authorisation.

Finally, if we consider that genetic data and bio-information used in scientific research often assume vast quantities, it must be conceded that the only way to process them effectively is by way of a computer program. But computer programs work with files, files are made of format (a set of instructions that allow the software to extract information from a file), and format can be copyrighted:

> Increasingly, genetic information is stored in formats other than a flat-file (readable by any software) and therefore requires, in order to be processed, the use of a specific computer program capable of reading those formats. It follows that those who own the copyright on the format in which the genetic information has been stored at the moment of the first digitalisation, as a matter of fact become its exclusive owner.[58]

The frightening consequence of the application of copyright to bio-information is that it becomes possible to circumvent the problem of the legal nature of the genetic information and the related matters of data protection and the right to privacy.

Does the right to control personal information override the copyright of a researcher? Are we to allow 'pirated' bio-information hidden in obscure and esoteric computer formats access to a treasure trove of knowledge – in the same way as a 14-year old Mozart allegedly memorised and then transcribed Gregorio Allegri's secret choral composition, *Miserere*, after hearing it performed once on a visit to the Vatican? Does information want to be free?

---

[58] Andrea Monti, 'Bioinformatica e diritto d'autore. La conoscenza ha bisogno di codici aperti' (2006) 7(4) *Ciberspazio e Diritto ascicolo* 533. English translation by Andrea Monti.

6

Personal Information and the Media

I. Introduction

The dissemination of personal information, particularly of celebrities, is the lifeblood of the tabloid press. Towards the end of the nineteenth century the convergence of a new technology (the portable Kodak camera) and the precursor of a social network (the tabloid newspapers) exploited individuals' appetite for gossip. The advent of the Internet and, as has occurred in the past, the emergence of a new reality-freezing technology in the form of digital still and video cameras have, of course, increased that appetite, and generate challenges beyond the wildest nightmares of Warren and Brandeis and, more importantly, raised questions about their concept of privacy.

Furthermore, the blurring of the (once clear) line between professional information and personal musings or rants, as well as the loss of centrality of the traditional information delivery platforms (printed magazines, television and radio broadcasting), allowed information to slip from the hands of those that once exerted a firm grip on it.

This chapter considers the law's efforts to protect the victims of media misconduct in regard to respect for private and family life, privacy, and other fundamental rights, and the difficulty of dealing with huge, individual minor infringements committed by single individuals. Its emphasis is on the manner in which both the Strasbourg and English courts have applied Article 8 of the ECHR. The experience of other jurisdictions has, where relevant, also been considered. The central argument, not surprisingly, is that greater precision is required in respect of the definition of 'privacy', 'private information', 'private life' and the 'public interest.'

Article 8 protects the 'right to respect for … private and family life, [and] … home.' Its reach has opened the gates to a considerable range of activities. While the language of the Article is considerably wider than a 'right to privacy', the judicial interpretation of it has inflated it even further. Thus the European Court has construed it to include a wide range of activities including 'aspects of an individual's physical and social identity;[1] the 'physical and psychological integrity

---

[1] *Pretty v United Kingdom* Application no 2346/02, (2002) 35 EHRR 1 at [61].

of a person';[2] the protection of the environment;[3] and 'the protection of personal autonomy.'[4]

The scale of this construction provides inadequate guidance both to the individual and the media in regard to their respective rights and obligations in this fundamental sphere of democratic freedom that, unfortunately, remains to be clearly defined judicially or legislatively.

The media are routinely chastised for their misbehaviour. The activities of the paparazzi are frequently denounced, and the tabloid press attracts censure. In the words of the Leveson Inquiry Report into press conduct in Britain:

> The evidence placed before the Inquiry has demonstrated, beyond any doubt, that there have been far too many occasions over the last decade and more (itself said to have been better than previous decades) when these responsibilities, on which the public so heavily rely, have simply been ignored. There have been too many times when, chasing the story, parts of the press have acted as if its own code, which it wrote, simply did not exist. This has caused real hardship and, on occasion, wreaked havoc with the lives of innocent people whose rights and liberties have been disdained. This is not just the famous but ordinary members of the public, caught up in events (many of them, truly tragic) far larger than they could cope with but made much, much worse by press behaviour that, at times, can only be described as outrageous.[5]

It will be contended that, if 'privacy' continues to be conceived as an amorphous cluster of interests – some with only a tenuous association with the fundamental concept of privacy (ie the protection of personal information) – the judicial interpretation of the law is likely to become increasingly uncertain, with negative consequences for both privacy and the media. The richness of this construction is simultaneously its poverty.[6] It resembles the nebulousness of the 'right to be let alone.'

But, as already argued, there is an important distinction between 'privacy' and 'private life'. The former relates to the right of an individual to control access to, or the publication or dissemination of, personal information. The latter is considerably wider, and concerns an individual's very being. As the Strasbourg Court has declared:

> It covers the physical and psychological integrity of a person. It can sometimes embrace aspects of an individual's physical and social identity. Elements such as, for

---

[2] See, for example, *Pretty v United Kingdom* (n 1 above); *YF v Turkey* Application 24209/94, (2004) 39 EHRR 34 at [33]. This includes the right to reputation, see *Pfeifer v Austria* Application no 12556/03, (2007) 48 EHRR 175 at [35]. This curious interpretation is considered below.

[3] See *Lopez Ostra v Spain* Application no 16798/90, (1995) 20 EHRR 277 at [51].

[4] *Goodwin v United Kingdom* Application no 28957/95, (2002) EHRR 18 at [90].

[5] *An Inquiry into the Culture, Practices and Ethics of the Press*, HC 780 (November 2012), Executive Summary, para 7, p 4. https://assets.publishing.service.gov.uk/government/uploads/system/uploads/attachment_data/file/229039/0779.pdf. The Inquiry examined only superficially the role of the Internet. In *Australian Broadcasting Corporation v Lenah Game Meats Pty Ltd* [2001] HCA 63 at [183] Kirby J declared: 'The power of the modern media, so important for the freedoms enjoyed in Australia, can sometimes be abused. When that happens, the courts are often the only institutions in our society with the power and the will to provide protection and redress to those who are gravely harmed.'

[6] Raymond Wacks, 'The Poverty of "Privacy"' (1980) 96 *Law Quarterly Review* 73.

example, gender identification, name and sexual orientation and sexual life fall within the personal sphere protected by Article 8. Article 8 also protects a right to personal development, and the right to establish and develop relationships with other human beings and the outside world. Although no previous case has established as such any right to self-determination as being contained in Article 8 of the Convention, the Court considers that the notion of personal autonomy is an important principle underlying the interpretation of its guarantees.[7]

While it makes sense to regard 'privacy' as a component of respect for 'private life', the breathtakingly broad compass of this conception moves well beyond any sensible idea of 'privacy'. Nor is this surprising, for Article 8 (despite the manner in which has been interpreted) does not purport to protect 'privacy'. At most, it protects the right to *respect* for privacy.[8] From a legal standpoint, its scope is unacceptably voluminous.

This muddies the question of what constitutes the type of information that warrants legal protection. If 'privacy' is a general right of this kind, it is important to declare in advance some conception of personal information; this is precisely what both the individual and the media need to know.

Lord Nicholls' caveat in *Campbell v MGN*, though it purports to circumscribe the concept of 'private life', relates only to the application of the test of 'reasonable expectation of privacy'. This perpetuates the confusion between the two domains. It does not attempt to identify what species of *personal information* are worthy of protection:

> Accordingly, in deciding what was the ambit of an individual's 'private life' in particular circumstances courts need to be on guard against using as a touchstone a test which brings into account considerations which should more properly be considered at the later stage of proportionality. Essentially the touchstone of private life is whether in respect of the disclosed facts the person in question had a reasonable expectation of privacy.[9]

But the test of proportionality is *already* applied when the court decides whether to grant an interim injunction. In other words, prior to issuing an injunction to halt publication, a court will necessarily attempt to balance the rival rights expressed in Articles 8 and 10. This requires an assessment of whether the public interest in publication (or the extent to which the disclosure contributes to a debate of general interest in a democratic society: see below) is proportionate to its effect on the claimant's right to respect of his private life; hence to privacy. Besides, the five-stage test adopted by the House of Lords, set out below, involves a dual application of the test of proportionality or what Lord Steyn called 'the ultimate balancing test.'[10]

[7] *Pretty v United Kingdom* [2002] 35 EHRR 1, [2002] ECHR 427 at [61].
[8] See *M v Secretary of State for Work and Pensions* [2006] 2 AC 91 at [83] per Lord Walker; *R (Gillan) v Commissioner of Police for the Metropolis* [2006] 2 AC 307 at [28] per Lord Bingham.
[9] *Campbell v Mirror Group Newspapers* [2004] UKHL 22 at [21], [2004] 2 AC 457.
[10] *Re S (A Child)* [2005] 1 AC 593 at [17]. It is sometimes described as 'parallel analysis': *A Local Authority v W* [2006] 1 FLR 1 at [53].

A better approach would be Gleeson CJ's 'highly offensive' test; it offers a sound, pragmatic method by which to differentiate between potentially serious violations of the claimant's privacy and those that are at the trivial end of the continuum.[11]

Given this generous view of the scope of Article 8, it may not be hard to see why it has been construed to include the protection of reputation.[12] Article 10 does, of course, provide explicit protection for an individual's reputation. Nevertheless the European Court of Human Rights has stated that, despite this, Article 8 may be engaged where the allegations against the applicant are 'of such a seriously offensive nature … [that they have] an inevitable direct effect on the applicant's private life.'[13] And an English court has followed suit:

> The protection of reputation is the primary function of the law of defamation. But although the ambit of the right of privacy is wider, it provides an alternative means of protecting reputation which is available even when the matters published are true … A party is entitled to invoke the right of privacy to protect his reputation.[14]

More recently, in *Cliff Richard v BBC*, Mann J was categorical:

> It is therefore quite plain that the protection of reputation is part of the function of the law of privacy as well the function of the law of defamation. That is entirely rational. As is obvious to anyone acquainted with the ways of the world, reputational harm can arise from matters of fact which are true but within the scope of a privacy right.[15]

Can this be correct? It may pass muster as an understanding of 'private life', but an infringement of privacy is sufficiently different from an attack on an individual's reputation to warrant a clear separation.

> The mental injuries suffered by a privacy plaintiff stem from exposure of his or her inner self to public view. The mental injuries suffered by a defamation victim, by contrast, arise as a consequence of the damage to reputation, either real or perceived, suffered in his or her public or private social circles. Thus, both torts provide redress for 'wounded feelings,' but the *source* of the harm differs substantially.[16]

Moreover, while there is an evident overlap between the two wrongs, in the case of defamation 'the injuries result from real or imagined harm to reputation, an objectively determinable interest. In privacy actions the injuries arise solely from public exposure of private facts.'[17]

---

[11] *Australian Broadcasting Corporation v Lenah Game Meats Pty Ltd* [2001] HCA 63, (2001) 185 ALR 1 at [42]. But see the differing views of the so-called Gleeson test by the court in *Campbell*, n 9 above.

[12] *Pfeifer v Austria* Application no 12556/03, (2007) 48 EHRR 175. A similar conclusion was reached by the court in *A v Norway* [2009] ECHR 580, *Radio France v France* Application no 53984/00, (2005) 40 EHRR 29. Cf *Axel Springer v Germany* Application no 39954/08, (2012) 55 EHRR 6 where the court looked for a 'certain level of seriousness and in a manner causing prejudice to personal enjoyment of the right to respect for private life,' at [83].

[13] *Karakó v Hungary* [2009] ECHR 712. See too *Petrenco v Moldova* [2010] ECHR 419.

[14] *Khuja v Times Newspapers Ltd* [2017] UKSC 49, [2017] 3 WLR 351 at [34].

[15] *Cliff Richard v British Broadcasting Corporation*, [2018] EWHC 1837 (Ch) at [345].

[16] Note, 'Defamation, Privacy and the First Amendment' (1976) *Duke Law Journal* 1016.

[17] ibid, 1034. See Tugendhat J's analysis of the 'limited classes of cases that the law of privacy gives rise to an overlap with the law of defamation' in *LNS (John Terry) v Persons Unknown* [2010] EWHC 119 (QB); [2010] EMLR 16 at [96].

Moreover, the well-developed defences to an action in defamation to protect free speech risk being undermined if such cases are pleaded under Article 8. Is Article 10's protection of freedom of expression (that may be overridden only by other rights – including the right to reputation – when necessary in a democratic society) an adequate safeguard when an action is brought under Article 8?

II. Defining the Media

In what we might call the Ink Age, newspapers and periodicals constituted what Burke dubbed the Fourth Estate.[18] The advent of broadcast and interactive media, especially Internet-based platforms, has greatly expanded the notion to include an almost unlimited number of individuals and groups with online access: non-profit media organisations, academics, bloggers and so on. Yet, despite this explosion in the quantity of voices in our Digital Age, the professional's institutional role remains – at least in the near future – largely the same: it performs a vital role in a democratic society. This 'Networked Fourth Estate':

> marks the emergence of a new model of watchdog function, one that is neither purely networked nor purely traditional, but is rather a mutualistic [sic] interaction between the two. It identifies the peculiar risks to, and sources of resilience of, the networked fourth estate in a multidimensional system of expression and restraint, and suggests the need to resolve a major potential vulnerability – the ability of private infrastructure companies to restrict speech without being bound by the constraints of legality, and the possibility that government actors will take advantage of this affordance in an extralegal public-private partnership for censorship … [I]t offers a richly detailed event study of the complexity of the emerging networked fourth estate, and the interaction, both constructive and destructive, between the surviving elements of the traditional model and the emerging elements of the new.[19]

This new reality has obvious implications for attempts to control or regulate the information machine. It also has wider constitutional significance in respect of the exercise of freedom of expression. The digital content-sharing networked platform constitutes a continuum with individual posters at one end, and 'heavyweight' media organisations at the other. In the middle reside a multitude of amateur and professional websites providing 'news', information and comment. It is no simple matter to determine which of these sources qualify as publishers that warrant

---

[18] Julianne Schultz, *Reviving the Fourth Estate* (Cambridge: Cambridge University Press, 1998) 49. See generally Paul Starr, *The Creation of the Media: Political Origins of Modern Communications* (New York: Basic Books, 2004).

[19] Yochai Benkler, 'A Free Irresponsible Press: Wikileaks and the Battle over the Soul of the Networked Fourth Estate' (2011) 46 *Harvard Civil Rights-Civil Liberties Law Review* 311, 396–97. This shift has not escaped the attention of the courts. See, for instance, *Commissioner of Police of the Metropolis v Times Newspapers Ltd* [2011] EWHC 2705 (QB), [2014] EMLR 1 at 127 per Tugendhat J. See too *Youth Initiative for Human Rights v Serbia* Application no 48135/06, (2013) 36 BHRC 687, quoted by Jacob Rowbottom, *Media Law* (Oxford: Hart Publishing, 2018) 28. See the discussion of the distinction between the institutional and functional definitions of the media, 27–31.

protection in the name of free speech. But does this question still make sense? Why should a 'publisher' be entitled to stronger legal protection than an individual expressing his or her views on a blog? The reduced significance of the ownership of the means of publishing and sharing (rotaries, printing machinery, newspaper delivery network etc), in favour of (almost) free digital content delivery creation and distribution tools, has blurred the line between professional journalism and information circulated by individuals. The medium is no longer the message; and the message is entitled to free speech protection, no matter (who owns) the medium.

It has therefore been suggested that the defining characteristic ought not to be the nature of the institution, but the function it performs in serving the interests of its users. Where it appears that an organ is carrying out journalistic activities, the argument goes, it should be regarded as part of the media and accorded the protection of the mainstream media.[20] It follows that such bodies ought also to be subject to the appropriate regulation.[21] It is clear, however, that while the nature of the media has been radically transformed and is subject to the vicissitudes of technology and society, free speech and freedom of information rights should be neither hampered nor constrained by the outdated distinction between information published by professionals and ordinary individuals.

This is important in regard to personal information because by rejecting the distinction between the 'information professional' and an individual information sharer it is possible to adopt a more coherent approach when considering the right to privacy. In fact, from a privacy perspective, such a distinction has not been drawn. The former has enjoyed not only the legal right to maintain the secrecy of its sources, but also the reluctance of the state to censor its publications or to seize a publication by way of court order. Similarly, individuals have the right to freedom of expression and, therefore, to whistle-blow public or private wrongdoing. In respect of civil liability, however, neither a journalist nor an individual is free to misuse another's personal information.

III. Collecting and Communicating

The principal focus of this chapter is the use to which personal information is put by the news media. In simple terms, it assumes two forms: first the collecting,

---

[20] This approach was adopted by the European Court of Human Rights in *Steel and Morris v United Kingdom* Application no 68416/01, (2005) 41 EHRR 22 at [89].

[21] See, for example, *Medžlis Islamske Zajednice Brčko v Bosnia and Herzegovina* Application no 17224/11 [2017] ECHR 608 in which the Grand Chamber of the European Court of Human Rights (somewhat surprisingly) treated an NGO that made certain allegations against a state body – but did not publish them beyond a letter to the authority in question – as a journalist, and therefore bound by obligations imposed on journalists. In *R v Marine A* [2013] EWCA Crim 2367, [2014] 1 WLR 3326 the Court held that the media's freedom of expression is founded on 'journalistic activity', not on the nature of the institution in question.

and, secondly, in most cases, the publication or communication of the information acquired. From a legal standpoint, these activities may conveniently be labelled, following William Prosser,[22] 'intrusion upon seclusion or solitude, or into private affairs', and 'public disclosure of embarrassing private facts'. Needless to say, these two activities are frequently inextricably linked. The media generally intrudes in order to publish the fruits of its invasion. The Peeping Tom's intrusion, however, typically proceeds no further.

But there is also a third possibility. The gathering of information already publicised by individuals on social networking and other networked user-generated content platforms: an activity that has become a regular operating procedure for journalists, who routinely access personal pages to collect pictures, videos and, more importantly, information about a person and his or her connections or opinions.

When I post something in a restricted circle, the information that is meant to be disclosed to members of the circle may not be secret, but is restricted. This shares the characteristics of e-mail, and has the same legal status (privileged) and protection (forbidding the illicit collection and further circulation.) If somebody, unbeknown to me, re-posts my original message, he or she is moving it outside the private space and may cause harm. But this is not always an infringement of the right to control personal information because what has been re-shared does not necessarily fall within the definition of personal information.

This distinction is helpful in providing guidance on assessing media behaviour: if information is shared publicly by the individual to whom it belongs, it falls within the journalist's prerogative to use it. If the information is publicly available but has been re-shared, the journalist should not assume that the information is – from a legal standpoint – to be treated in the same way as in the first case. If the information is not public and the journalist takes it by requesting contact without revealing his or her status, this constitutes a violation of Article 8, even though it does not involve a threat to personal information.

In the case of intrusion, the obtaining of personal information by the media assumes a variety of forms, from the simple interview to sophisticated surreptitious electronic surveillance and covert photography.[23] Like DNA (which is

[22] William L Prosser, 'Privacy' (1960) 48 *California Law Review* 383. Cf Neil M Richards and Daniel J Solove, 'Prosser's Privacy Law: A Mixed Legacy' (2010) 98 *California Law Review* 1887.

[23] The Strasbourg Court has held that monitoring an individual in a public place by the use of photographic equipment without recording such data does not, as such, give rise to an interference with the individual's private life, but the *recording* of the data and the systematic or permanent nature of the record may generate such considerations: *Perry v United Kingdom* Application no 63737/00, (2004) 39 EHRR 37 at [38]. It has found several cases of 'intrusion' to be a breach of Article 8: *Wood v United Kingdom* Application no 23414/02 (judgment of 20 January 2004), *Khan v United Kingdom*, Application no 35394/97, (2001) 31 EHRR 45, *Allan v United Kingdom* Application no 48539/99, (2003) 36 EHRR 12 (bugging); *Halford v United Kingdom* Application no 20605/92 (1997) 24 EHRR 523, *Amman v Switzerland* Application no 27798/95, (2000) 30 EHRR 843, *Huvig v France* Application no 11105/84, (1990) 12 EHRR 528, *Doerga v Netherlands* Application no 50210, (2005) 41 EHRR 4 (telephone tapping); *Peck v United Kingdom* Application no 44647/98, (2003) 36 EHRR 719, *Perry v United*

a chemical compound from which genetic information, can be gleaned) a photograph is not in and of itself personal information; it is a 'carrier' of information.[24] But the mere taking of a photograph does not necessarily constitute a breach of Article 8 or of the General Data Protection Regulation (GDPR).[25] However, the publication of an image of a person which, in the words of Lord Hoffmann, 'reveals him to be in a situation of humiliation or severe embarrassment, even if taken in a public place, may be an infringement of the privacy of his personal information.'[26] And 'the fact that we cannot avoid being photographed does not mean that anyone who takes or obtains such photographs can publish them to the world at large.'[27] But, again, as argued in Chapter five, this has more to do with the violation of dignity, harassment and defamation than with the infringement of either a generalised right to privacy à la Warren and Brandeis or with the protection of personal information.

Where an individual is photographed in a public place, the thorny question arises as to whether the media may be liable for the image's capture or publication, or both.[28] At first blush, it would appear that the information acquired, since it is transacted in the public domain, cannot be 'personal'. Yet, as mentioned above, there may be circumstances in which the image exposes the individual to humiliation or embarrassment.[29] Moreover, a number of factors will fall to be considered,

---

Kingdom, above (unauthorised or unwarranted videoing); *Wainwright v United Kingdom* Application no 12350/04, (2007) 44 EHRR 40 (intimate body searches).

[24] 'Nor is it right to treat a photograph simply as a means of conveying factual information. A photograph can certainly capture every detail of a momentary event in a way which words cannot, but a photograph can do more than that. A personal photograph can portray, not necessarily accurately, the personality and the mood of the subject of the photograph.' *Douglas v Hello! (No 3)* [2005] EWCA Civ 595, [2006] QB 125 at [106] per Lord Phillips MR. In *Von Hannover v Germany* the Strasbourg Court stated that the 'publication of photos … is an area in which the protection of the rights and reputation of others takes on particular importance. The present case does not concern the dissemination of "ideas", but of *images containing very personal or even intimate "information" about an individual':* *Von Hannover v Germany* Application no 59320/00 (2005) 40 EHRR 1 at [59], quoted in *Douglas* at [87], and endorsed in *Von Hannover v Germany (No 2)* Applications nos 40660/08 and 60641/08 [2012] ECHR 228, at [103].

[25] *Campbell v Mirror Group Newspapers* [2004] UKHL 22, [2004] 2 AC 457 at [73]; *Murray v Express Newspapers plc* [2009] Ch 481 at [54]; *Wood v Commissioner of Police for the Metropolis* [2010] EMLR 1 (CA) at [36]; *Theakston v Mirror Group Newspapers* [2002] EWHC 137 (QB), [2002] EMLR 22.

[26] *Campbell,* n 25 above, at [75]. This is an important recognition that to warrant protection the photograph must contain or convey personal or intimate information. But compare *Reklos v Greece* Application no 1234/05 (2009) 27 BHRC 420 where the Strasbourg Court held that Greece had contravened Article 8 for failing to provide a remedy for a photograph of a newborn taken without the consent of its parents. This is a step too far.

[27] *Campbell,* n 25 above, at [74]. See *Peck v United Kingdom,* Application no 44647/98 (2003) 36 EHRR 41 where an individual was filmed on a public street in an embarrassing moment by a CCTV camera. The images were subsequently broadcast several times on TV. The Strasbourg Court held that Article 8 had been breached.

[28] For a penetrating analysis of the problem, see NA Moreham, 'Privacy in Public Places' (2006) 65 *Cambridge Law Journal* 606.

[29] *Peck v United Kingdom,* Application no 44647/98, (2003) 36 EHRR 719 (filming of a suicide attempt in a public place).

including whether the image was obtained covertly,[30] and the nature of the activity in which the individual was engaged.[31]

Strangely enough, the assessment of the legal status of public photography and videography – whether overt or covert – is usually focused on the contrast between freedom of information and a confused amalgam of the right to privacy and the right to protection of one's image. What is often overlooked in this context are the rights of an author as expressed, in particular, in Article 2 of the Berne Convention for the Protection of Literary and Artistic Works, which accords photography the status of a work of art.[32]

The Tribunal de Grande Instance de Paris, in two leading decisions,[33] considered this matter. In the first,[34] it held that candid photographs taken in the Paris underground by Luc Delahaye, a photographer and member of the international agency Magnum, and published in his book *L'autre*,[35] were legitimate because of the artistic and cultural aims pursued by the author, expressed in a manner non-harmful to the people portrayed.[36] The second case, known as *La dame au petit chien* (the lady with the little dog)[37] involved a claim by a woman who had been photographed candidly and the picture published in a book by the French novelist and photographer, François-Marie Banier.[38] According to the French Court, the bare facts captured by the photographer showed a woman with her dog, seated on a public bench and talking on her phone. Although she was alone, it did not follow that she was in an intimate situation.[39] The court held that her position, taken as a whole, the presence of a pet at her side, or her choice of apparel were merely anodyne facts about her that were not relevant to the domain protected by Article 9 of the Civil Code as respect for private life.

The French Supreme Court has unequivocally accepted that anodyne facts are not related to private life and the Chambre d'Appel de Paris has made clear that only a public interest in personal information can override the right to respect for private life.

There has, however, been an unfortunate tendency to expand the scope of Article 8 to include conduct in public that cannot be characterised as 'personal'.

---

[30] *Von Hannover v Germany*, Application no 59320/00, (2005) 40 EHRR 1.
[31] *Douglas v Hello! (No 3)* [2005] EWCA Civ 595, [2006] QB 125.
[32] On the political role of photography, see, in particular, Susan Sontag, *Regarding the Pain of Others* (London: Penguin, 2003). Cf Ariella Azoulay, *Civil Imagination: A Political Ontology of Photography* (London: Verso Books, 2015).
[33] Agnès Tricoire, 'Les œuvres et les visages: la liberté de création s'affirme contre le droit à la vie privée et le droit à l'image', commentaire de Tribunal de Grande Instance Paris 17e ch. 09/05/2007 et 25/06/2007, Dalloz 2008, n° 1, p 57.
[34] Tribunal de Grande Instance Paris, 2 juin 2004, Légipresse n° 214. septembre 2004.
[35] Luc Delahaye, *L'autre* (London: Phaidon Press, 1999).
[36] Tribunal de Grande Instance Paris, 2 juin 2004, Légipresse n° 214. septembre 2004, 156.
[37] Tribunal de Grande Instance Paris, 17e ch, 16 November 2006, Légipresse n° 240.
[38] François-Marie Banier, *Perdre la tête* (Paris: Gallimard, 2006).
[39] Agnès Tricoire, n 33 above.

The Strasbourg Court's *Von Hannover* decision[40] afforded a signal that has been followed in a number of English cases.[41] The connection to 'privacy' in some of these decisions is, at best, questionable, especially where the images are published online. Remedies for the collection and dissemination of images might find a more appropriate, congenial home in data protection laws.[42]

In this regard, though, the GDPR sets a clear limit to the protection of personal data in relation to the freedom of speech and of information. Article 17 is unequivocal in affirming that the so-called right to be forgotten cannot be invoked against those human rights.

But the enforcement of the GDPR as a legal remedy against this activity poses various difficulties. Consider the candid photograph taken in 1957 in Caracas by the Colombian photographer, Leo Matiz, *Magda and the Dwarf*. It was candid in the classic, Henry Cartier-Bresson-like street-photography style, and was acquired by the New York Museum of Modern Art.

The name of the woman portrayed in the picture remained unknown for 35 years. Only in 1992 did she recognise herself when she saw the picture hanging on the wall of an exhibition in Milan. According to the highly questionable interpretation of both the former EU Data Protection Directive and the GDPR, this picture should neither have been taken (in the EU) nor exposed nor released online because of the lack of consent to its taking and publication.[43]

The 'cultural aim' exception recognised by French jurisprudence represents a powerful argument against the creation of a tort as a direct, automatic consequence of taking and sharing a (candidly taken) photograph. Adding the French cultural exception into the balancing of rights needed to assess whether a certain type of photography is unlawful renders the decision more complicated. A viable solution may be found in the American tort of intrusion, where a test is applied that includes the offensiveness of the defendant's intrusive act. The wrong consists in the intentional interference with the plaintiff's solitude or seclusion, such as physical intrusion into the plaintiff's premises, or eavesdropping (eg, electronic and photographic surveillance, bugging and telephone hacking and tapping).

---

[40] *Von Hannover* (n 24 above) (Article 8 was held to be engaged despite the images revealing mundane, non-private activities).

[41] *Weller v Associated Newspapers Ltd* [2015] EWCA Civ 1176, [2016] 1 WLR 1541 (publication of photographs of children of a pop star in a public place breached Article 8). See too *Murray v Express Newspapers PLC* [2008] EWCA Civ 446, [2009] Ch 481.

[42] See *Eastweek Publisher Ltd v Privacy Commissioner for Personal Data* [2000] HKC 692; Raymond Wacks, *Law, Morality, and the Private Domain* (Hong Kong: Hong Kong University Press, 2000) 12–16; Raymond Wacks, 'What has Data Protection to do with Privacy?' (2000) 6 *Privacy Law and Policy Reporter* 143. See Chapter 2 of this volume.

[43] *Magda and the Dwarf* is an example of how it is possible to distort the meaning of the GDPR. Henry Cartier-Bresson, Gerry Winongrad, Vivian Meier, Daido Moryama, Vittorugo Contino, Caio Mario Garrubba, Calogero Cascio and the thousands of lesser-known street photographers around the world devoted their careers to freezing un-staged moments of life, preserving history and leaving a legacy for posterity. Thankfully, Leo Matiz and the other street photographers of the past did not have their freedom curtailed by the likes of the GDPR.

Three requirements must be met: (a) there must be actual prying, (b) the intrusion must be such as would offend a reasonable man, and (c) it must be an intrusion into something private. This is succinctly captured by the gloss of the *American Restatement*:

> One who intentionally intrudes, physically or otherwise, upon the solitude or seclusion of another or his private affairs or concerns, is subject to liability to the other for invasion of his privacy, if the intrusion would be highly offensive to a reasonable person.

Its comment reads in part:

> The form of invasion of privacy … does not depend upon any publicity given to the person whose interest is invaded or to his affairs. It consists solely of an intentional interference with his interest in solitude or seclusion, either as to his person or as to his private affairs or concerns, of a kind that would be highly offensive to a reasonable man.[44]

IV. 'Reasonable Expectation of Privacy'

This test is central to the intrusion tort.[45] Interpreting the Fourth Amendment, the United States Supreme Court has held that a person has a reasonable expectation of privacy if (a) he, by his conduct, has exhibited an actual (or subjective) expectation of privacy; that is, he has shown that he seeks to preserve something as private; and (b) his subjective expectation of privacy is one that society is prepared to recognise as reasonable; that is, the expectation, viewed objectively, is justifiable under the circumstances.[46]

An individual does not have a subjective expectation of privacy if he has been put on notice that his activities in a specified area will be watched by others for a legitimate purpose. In American tort law the factors determining the reasonableness of an expectation of privacy include: (a) whether the area is generally accessible to the public; (b) whether the individual has a property interest in the area; (c) whether the individual has taken normal precautions to maintain his privacy; (d) how the area is used; and (e) the general understanding of society that certain areas deserve the most scrupulous protection from intrusion.[47]

---

[44] *Restatement of the Law, Second, Torts*, para 652.

[45] Is it unduly pedantic to enquire what precisely the 'privacy' in this test actually means? No attempt is made, as far as one can tell, to elucidate what concept of 'privacy' one is supposed reasonably to expect. If it entails that the victim ought to expect the expansive notion of 'privacy' in the current nebulous interpretation of Article 8, the objective standard seems, to say the least, tenuous. If, on the other hand, as argued here, 'privacy' is confined to the obtaining or misuse of personal information, the test becomes a pragmatic assessment of legitimate anticipation, especially in the case of intrusion. See below.

[46] *Smith v Maryland* 442 US 735 (1979). See too *Illinois v Caballes* 543 US 405 (2005); *Huskey v National Broadcasting Co* 632 F Supp 1282 (ND Ill 1986); *Sanders v ABC* 20 Cal 4th 907, 85 Cal Rptr 2d 909, 978 P 2d 67; *United States v Jones* 132 S Ct 945 (2012).

[47] *Rakas v Illinois* 439 US 128 (1978), 152–53; *Oliver v United States*, 466 US 170 (1984), 178–83.

The concept of 'reasonable expectation of privacy' is thus at the heart of the American tort of intrusion. The United States Supreme Court has held that a person has a reasonable expectation of privacy if (a) he, by his conduct, has exhibited an actual (or subjective) expectation of privacy; that is, he has shown that he seeks to preserve something as private; and (b) his subjective expectation of privacy is one that society is prepared to recognise as reasonable; that is, the expectation, viewed objectively, is justifiable under the circumstances.[48] Furthermore, the judicial source of the test involved the interception of telephone calls. It arose in the Supreme Court's decision in *Katz v United States*[49] which, interpreting the Fourth Amendment's protection against 'unreasonable searches and seizures',[50] held that in order to warrant protection, the plaintiff must have had a 'reasonable expectation of privacy.'[51]

This test has now been adopted by the English courts.[52] 'The first question is whether there is a reasonable expectation of privacy.'[53] The Master of the Rolls added that the question is a broad one which comprises all the circumstances of the case, including the attributes of the claimant, the nature of the activity in which the claimant was involved, the place at which it was happening, and the nature and purpose of the intrusion.[54] The test, the Court of Appeal explained, focuses on the

---

[48] *Smith v Maryland*, 442 US 735 (1979).See *Rakas v Illinois* 439 US 128 (1978), 152–53; *Oliver v United States* 466 US 170 (1984), 178–83.

[49] *Katz v United States* 389 US 347 (1967).

[50] The Fourth Amendment provides: 'The right of the people to be secure in their persons, houses, papers, and effects, against unreasonable searches and seizures, shall not be violated, and no Warrants shall issue, but upon probable cause, supported by Oath or affirmation, and particularly describing the place to be searched, and the persons or things to be seized.' In *United States v Jones* 565 US 400 (2012) the Supreme Court held that installing a GPS tracking device on a person's car and the use of that device to monitor the vehicle's movements on public streets, constitutes a search or seizure within the meaning of the Fourth Amendment and therefore required a search warrant.

[51] The Supreme Court famously stated that the Fourth Amendment 'protects people, not places.' What an individual knowingly exposes to the public, even in his home or office, is not protected by the Fourth Amendment. But what he or she seeks to preserve as private, even in an area accessible to the public, may be constitutionally protected.

[52] But not always by the Strasbourg Court. See, in particular, *Sciacca v Italy* Application no 50774/99, (2005) 43 EHRR 20 and *Reklos v Greece* Application no 1234/05 (2009) 27 BHRC 420. For the suggestion that the test is 'incoherent and redundant and it should … be discarded', see Eric Barendt, '"A Reasonable Expectation of Privacy": A Coherent or Redundant Concept?' in AT Kenyon (ed), *Comparative Defamation and Privacy Law* (Cambridge: Cambridge University Press, 2016) 96, 104–13. According to Lord Kerr, (*Re JR38's Application for Judicial Review* [2015] UKSC 42; [2015] EMLR 25) a rigorous application of the reasonable expectation test was incompatible with the jurisprudence of the Strasbourg Court on Article 8 of the ECHR, which is generally unconcerned whether the claimant had a reasonable expectation of privacy. See, for example, the decisions in *Sciacca v Italy* (above) (supply by the police to newspapers of a suspect's photographs and their publication engages Art 8) and in *Reklos v Greece* (taking of an infant's photograph in hospital without parental consent engages Art 8) or which sometimes treats it as only a factor to be taken into account in determining whether the right to respect for private life guaranteed by the Article is engaged. See the judgments of the European Human Rights Court in *PG v United Kingdom* (2008) 46 EHRR 51 at [57] and in *Von Hannover v Germany* (2005) 40 EHRR 1 at [51] considered in *Re JR38* at [38] and [84] respectively.

[53] *Murray v Express Newspapers plc* [2009] Ch 481 at [35] per Sir Anthony Clarke MR.

[54] *Murray*, at [36].

sensibilities of a reasonable person in the position of the victim when determining whether the conduct falls within the sphere of Article 8.

The test, however, is far from straightforward. Moreover, it sits less well in cases of public disclosure than those of intrusion. If I do not wish to be observed in my home, it would be reasonable to leave my curtains drawn. When I do not wish to be heard, it would be unreasonable for me to discuss private matters within earshot of others. My expectation of not being seen or heard is a function of the steps I take to protect my 'privacy'. In the case of disclosure, however, the determination of whether my expectation that I will not be exposed to publicity is reasonable is more complex.

Where my complaint is that I am being pursued by paparazzi using zoom lenses, or that I suspect I am the subject of surreptitious surveillance, or that my telephone is being tapped, my room or office is bugged, or my computer is hacked into, the question is correctly asked whether, in all the circumstances, I have a reasonable expectation of privacy.[55]

What does this mean? It provides an objective measure by which to decide whether I am entitled to assume that my personal information has not been exposed to unintended recipients. It therefore examines the *circumstances* rather than only the *information* that may warrant protection. Thus, when the Duchess of Cambridge, sunbathing nude beside the swimming pool on private premises, was photographed from a distance, was she reasonably entitled to expect that her privacy was secure? But of what precisely must she have had a reasonable expectation? That she would not be seen? By whom? That she would not be photographed with a long-lens camera? That, if photographed, the resulting images would not be published?

The focus on the *circumstances* surrounding the information, and in particular its unrestricted movement around the information ecosphere, may be a consideration in ascertaining the existence of a right to privacy, but it is neither the only nor the most important one. What matters most, as will be seen below, is that we need a pre-emptive categorisation of the information in question prior to claiming an infringement of the right to privacy.

French case law regards anodyne information about an individual as irrelevant in respect of protection of their privacy. It follows that the circulation of this sort of information is not harmful per se. By contrast, when such information is of an intimate and personal nature, sharing it falls to be considered as a possible violation of privacy.

The last question shifts the enquiry to the *misuse* of the personal information thereby garnered. In this situation, the 'reasonable expectation' test on its own may be insufficient because it raises different concerns that relate to the *use* to which

---

[55] See Nicole Moreham, 'Privacy in the Common Law: A Doctrinal and Theoretical Analysis' (2005) 121 *Law Quarterly Review* 628, 643–44; and 'Beyond Information: Physical Privacy in English Law' (2014) 73 *Cambridge Law Journal* 350.

the victim is willing to consent. It is, in other words, a matter of *control* over the broadcasting of personal information. By conflating the two violations, the analysis not only neglects the separate interests of the victim that are generated by each activity, but it also complicates the balancing exercise with Article 10 that arises in cases of disclosure.[56]

These questions have been carefully considered by the Italian Supreme Court in a couple of landmark decisions. In its ruling 40577/2008 it held:

> A third party violates privacy and commits a crime under Section 615-bis Criminal Code, if the object of the photograph is conduct hidden from normal visibility, since the protection of private space is granted only to what is done in such conditions as are not visible to the general public. Thus, if an event happens in a private place but can be freely seen without a particular aid [a telephoto lens, for instance] the owner of the private space cannot reasonably expect his privacy to be respected.[57]

Two years later, in ruling 47165/2010, the Court went further, stating:

> It is necessary to balance the privacy need (rooted in the Constitution as an expression of the individual personality and as protection of private space …) and the natural limitation of this right as derived from the specific factual situation and, furthermore, the tacit, but unequivocal – withdrawal of this right that occurs in the case of a person who, while using a private space, locates himself in a position that renders him visible to a plurality of persons.

Finally in 2015 in a case involving Silvio Berlusconi, the Supreme Court reaffirmed the above-mentioned principles, but explained that the use of a long lens and image manipulation software to magnify the pictures were evidence that what was taking place in his villa was intended to be hidden from public view and that, therefore, a privacy infringement had been committed.[58] Before taking into account the circumstances of the shooting of the pictures (use of a telephoto lens to circumvent the villa's walls), the Supreme Court stated that it is not relevant that the individuals portrayed were photographed in those outdoor parts of the villa that, although they were protected by its walls from an observer at ground level, were visible from a higher vantage point by the use of a telephoto lens. This fact did not weaken their right to privacy because the presence of the wall was a clear message not to gaze into the property. But the Court went further and extended its reach to analyse the role of software technologies (photograph retouching applications) used to magnify small images or part of them, to render them suitable for publication and gossip. Using software to extract (or, as in this case, to enhance) information not otherwise easily accessible gives rise to a legitimate privacy claim.

---

[56] See Raymond Wacks, *Privacy and Media Freedom* (Oxford: Oxford University Press, 2013), especially chapters 4, 5, and 8.
[57] Corte Suprema di cassazione Ruling N° 40577/2008.
[58] Corte di cassazione Seconda Sezione Penale, sentenza 25363/2015.

The difference is between the victim's *expectation* in the case of *intrusion*, and his or her *wishes* in respect of *disclosure*.[59] The two are often closely connected, but not ineluctably so. It is perfectly plausible for a celebrity to object to her photograph being taken surreptitiously, but content to permit its publication by the media. Even if her dissatisfaction applies to both, however, the wrongfulness of the intrusion properly turns on her reasonable expectation of privacy, while the unlawfulness of the subsequent publication should be decided by reference to her right to control the use or misuse of her image.[60]

The approach suggested here is that in cases of unwanted publicity, a court, having established that the information in question was indeed 'personal', should identify the specific interests and features of the person that the law seeks to protect.[61] So, for example, where the media obtain personal information to harass or blackmail an individual[62] or where it is acquired surreptitiously,[63] the courts have shown little sympathy for the press.

---

[59] The significance of the victim's wishes occurs in two attempts to conceptualise 'privacy'. Moreham includes the element of 'desire' when defining privacy as '[T]he state of "desired inaccess" or as "freedom from unwanted access". In other words, a person will be in a state of privacy if he or she is only seen, heard, touched or found out about if, and to the extent that, he or she wants to be seen, heard, touched or found out about. Something is therefore "private" if a person has a desire for privacy in relation to it: a place, event or activity will be "private" if a person wishes to be free from outside access when attending or undertaking it and information will be "private" if the person to whom it relates does not want people to know about it'. Nicole Moreham, 'Privacy in the Common Law: A Doctrinal and Theoretical Analysis" (n 55 above) 636. And Solove writes to similar effect when he argues that privacy 'involves more than avoiding disclosure; it also involves the individual's ability to ensure that personal information is used for the purposes she desires.' D Solove, 'Conceptualizing Privacy' (2002) 90 *California Law Review* 1087, 1108. See too D Solove, 'A Taxonomy of Privacy' (2006) 154 *University of Pennsylvania Law Review* 477.

[60] There are a few judgments in which a severance is espoused. In *Wood v Commissioner of Police for the Metropolis* [2010] EMLR 1 (CA) at [33], Laws LJ distinguished between 'the fact or threat of publication in the media, and ... the snapping of the shutter.' A dichotomy of this kind was adopted also in *Theakston v Mirror Group Newspapers Ltd* [2002] EMLR 22, where the court drew a distinction between the intrusion into the claimant's sexual activities, on the one hand (which it did not protect) and the publication of photographs of him in a brothel (which it did), on the other. Moreover, in the leading authority, to which the courts routinely defer, *Von Hannover v Germany* [2004] EMLR 379 (ECHR), (2004) 40 EHRR 1 the European Court of Human Rights applied the 'reasonable expectation of privacy' test to the intrusive activities of the media, and not to the publication of the material so obtained. And it followed its earlier decision in *Halford v United Kingdom* (1997) 24 EHRR 523.

[61] See *Goodwin v News Group Newspapers Ltd* [2011] EWHC 1437 (QB), at [87]; *Trimingham v Associated Newspapers Limited* [2012] EWHC 1296 (QB). A similar approach was adopted by the Supreme Court in the judgment of Lord Kerr, although the case did not concern the misuse of personal information: *Re JR38's Application for Judicial Review* [2015] UKSC 42 at [39] and [53]. The learned judge referred to the claimant's age and the use to which the information would be put as factors to be taken into account when determining whether Article 8 was engaged. See too *Murray v Express Newspapers PLC* [2008] EWCA Civ 446, [2009] Ch 481 at [36].

[62] See *ZAM v CFW and TFW* [2013] EWHC 662 (QB), [2013] EMLR 27.

[63] See *TRK v ICM* [2016] EWHC 2810 (QB); *CTB v News Group Newspapers Ltd* [2011] EWHC 1326 (QB); *Gulati v Mirror Group Newspapers* [2015] EWCA Civ 1291, [2017] QB 149; *Tchenguiz v Imerman* [2010] EWCA Civ 908. Nevertheless, intrusion has not been recognized as a tort, despite several dicta that appear to support this development. See, for example *Gulati v MGN* [2015] EWHC 1482 (Ch), [2016] FSR 12 at [143]. See R Wacks, *Privacy and Media Freedom*, n 56 above, 246–47. Cf the decisions of the courts in New Zealand: *C v Holland* [2012] NZHC 2155, and Canada: *Jones v Tsige* [2012] ONCA 32. It has been described as 'physical privacy', see NA Moreham, 'Beyond Information: Physical

As argued throughout this work, the essence of our concern to protect the right to privacy is the interest in safeguarding of personal, sensitive information against its misuse. Although Article 8 employs the phrase 'private *life*' the courts have interpreted this notion to protect 'private *facts*' against unauthorised disclosure. The distinction is explained in Chapter two.

To repeat, courts ought first to establish whether the facts are genuinely personal, intimate or sensitive and thus worthy of legal protection.[64] Moreover, this approach would provide stronger protection to the media's exercise of freedom of expression. In other words, by focusing on the *categories* of personal information, rather than the *circumstances* that may give rise to a reasonable expectation of privacy, the law would send a clearer message – to both the media and the public – as to where the law draws the line between privacy and free speech.

V. 'Misuse of Personal Information'

The English law, since the enactment of the Human Rights Act in 1998, has undergone a major shift in its recognition of privacy under Article 8's protection of 'private life'. This provision has been integrated into domestic law; the innovative civil wrong: the 'misuse of personal information' now provides protection to an individual's 'private and family life, home and correspondence.' This is not a full-blown right to privacy,[65] although it is increasingly treated as one.[66]

When considering an action under Article 8, the English courts adopt a five-stage enquiry:

(1)   Is Article 8 engaged? If not, that is the end of the matter.
(2)   If Article 8 is engaged, is Article 10 also engaged?
(3)   If so, then the court will seek to 'balance' the competing rights, applying an 'intense focus' upon the facts to decide which article should yield.
(4)   Other rights (ECHR and non-ECHR) may need to be taken into account, and, in respect of the former, the same balancing approach should be adopted as is the case in respect of Article 10.
(5)   The 'balancing' process should avoid mere generalities.

Privacy in English Law' (2014) 73 *Cambridge Law Journal* 350. But is that really so? Surely, if 'privacy' is the complaint, the fundamental wrong resides less in the encroachment upon the victim's space than the attempt to obtain (or success in) acquiring personal information.

[64] See *TLU and others v Secretary of State for the Home Department* [2018] EWCA Civ 2217.

[65] The right enshrined in Article 8 is not a 'right to privacy', but a right to '*respect*' for privacy. See *M v Secretary of State for Work and Pensions* [2006] 2 AC 91 at [83] per Lord Walker; *R (Gillan) v Commissioner of Police for the Metropolis* [2006] 2 AC 307 at [28] per Lord Bingham.

[66] See *Campbell v MGN Ltd* [2004] 2 AC 457. The House of Lords in *Wainwright v Home Office* [2003] 3 WLR 1137 declared that 'there is no general tort of invasion of privacy'? [43]. In *McKennitt v Ash* [2006] EWCA Civ 1714, [2008] QB 73 at [11] Buxton LJ stated that Articles 8 and 10 'are the very content of the domestic tort.'

In pursuing the process in (5):

> It is well established in authority that in a case in which both Article 8 and Article 10 are engaged (and therefore likely to be pulling in different directions) that the court has to perform a balancing and weighing act to ascertain which predominates … As a matter of principle neither of them has primacy.[67]

The criteria to be adopted follow those articulated in the leading European decision, *Axel Springer*,[68] which involves a test expressed in the following six questions:

(a) Does the disclosure contribute to a debate of general interest?
(b) How well known is the person concerned, and what is the subject of the report?
(c) What was the prior conduct of the person concerned in regard to publicity?
(d) How was the information obtained, and is it true?
(e) What are the content, form and consequences of the publication?
(f) How severe was the sanction imposed on the applicant?

In *Trimingham v Associated Newspapers Limited*[69] the complainant's grievance was that the newspaper had, inter alia, published offensive articles about her appearance and sexuality. She claimed damages, including aggravated damages, and an injunction against the newspaper ordering them to refrain from referring to her sexual orientation unless relevant in a particular context distinct from her relationship with a politician and that the newspaper refrain from harassing the claimant. In the High Court, Tugendhat J stated, should ask: (1) was the distress suffered the result of the course of conduct, in the form of speech? (2) If so, ought the defendant to have known that the course of conduct amounted to harassment? (3) If so, has the defendant shown that the pursuit of that course of conduct was reasonable? To both questions (1) and (2) he added, there were secondary questions: namely, was the claimant a purely private figure, and was she in other respects a person with a personality known to the defendant such that it ought to have known that the course of conduct amounted to harassment?

In respect of the defence of reasonableness, Tugendhat J held that in order for the Court to comply with section 3 of the Human Rights Act, it must hold that a course of conduct in the form of journalistic speech is reasonable, unless it is so unreasonable that it is necessary (in the sense of a pressing social need) and proportionate to prohibit or sanction the speech in pursuit of one of the aims listed in Article 10(2) – including, in particular, the protection of the rights of others under Article 8. It concluded that the claimant was not a private person by reason of the fact because she worked for a leading politician, and she conducted a sexual

---

[67] *Cliff Richard v British Broadcasting Corporation* [2018] EWHC 1837 (Ch) at [270]. See generally *McKennitt v Ash* [2008] QB 73. This question is canvassed at length in R Wacks, *Privacy and Media Freedom*, n 56 above, chapter 5.
[68] *Axel Springer v Germany* Application no 39954/08, (2012) 55 EHRR 6.
[69] *Trimingham v Associated Newspapers Limited* [2012] EWHC 1296 (QB).

relationship with a politician which would result in his leaving his wife. The Court rejected the argument that the defendant ought to have known that its conduct would be sufficiently distressing to be considered oppressive or amount to harassment. Such a course of conduct might be unreasonable if it interfered with the Article 8 rights of the claimant.

The courts have demonstrated a salutary readiness to prevent brazen breaches of its authority. Thus, where a prominent footballer's name was revealed online, notwithstanding an interim injunction against *The Sun* preventing disclosure of their sexual relationship, Eady J refused to vary the terms of the injunction to permit the identification of the claimant. He distinguished his own decision in *Mosley v News Group Newspapers Ltd*[70] on the ground that the intimate video in that case had been seen by hundreds of thousands – even before the application for the order. Here, the disclosure of the footballer's identity occurred after the interim order had been granted.

The learned judge observed that a time might come when the information in question is so widely disseminated that there is nothing left for the law to protect. Nevertheless, he concluded that amending the order would engulf the claimant and his family

> in a cruel and destructive media frenzy. Sadly, that may become unavoidable in the society in which we now live but, for the moment, in so far as I am being asked to sanction it, I decline to do so. On the other side … it has not been suggested that there is *any* legitimate public interest in publishing the story.[71]

He added,

> It is fairly obvious that wall-to-wall excoriation in national newspapers, whether tabloid or 'broadsheet', is likely to be significantly more intrusive and distressing for those concerned than the availability of information on the Internet or in foreign journals to those, however many, who take the trouble to look it up. Moreover, with each exposure of personal information or allegations, whether by way of visual images or verbally, there is a new intrusion and occasion for distress or embarrassment. Mr Tomlinson argues accordingly that 'the dam has not burst'. For so long as the court is in a

---

[70] *Mosley v News Group Newspapers Ltd* [2008] EWHC 687 (QB). Soon after the claimant's identity was revealed in Parliament by an MP, a further application was made to Tugendhat J to lift the anonymity restriction on the ground that the footballer's name was now readily available. He declined to do so because the object of the injunction was not solely to protect private information, but to prevent intrusion and harassment of the claimant and his family. It was reported that the claimant has launched an action against Twitter Inc to disclose the identities of anonymous account holders alleged to have breached Eady J's injunction by revealing the claimant's identity: *CTB v Twitter, Inc. and Persons Unknown* (2012) Case No HQ11XO1814. Cf *PJS v News Group Newspapers Ltd* [2016] UKSC, [2016] AC 1081 where the Supreme Court, distinguishing *Mosley*, refused to discharge an injunction restricting the reporting of a public figure's 'three-way' homosexual antics with three men, despite the fact that that it had been widely publicised online. Whereas in *Mosley* the publication occurred *before* the application for an injunction, in *PJS* it happened after the injunction had been imposed.

[71] *CTB v News Group Newspapers Ltd* [2011] EWHC 1326 (QB) judgment of 23 May 2011, at [26].

position to prevent *some* of that intrusion and distress, depending upon the individual circumstances, it may be appropriate to maintain that degree of protection. The analogy with King Canute to some extent, therefore, breaks down.[72]

VI. The Public Interest

The boundaries that restrict the right to privacy are drawn by the right to publish information that contributes to a debate on a matter of general interest. The essential question is when personal information may be published on the ground that it is in the public interest.[73] In a democracy, the answer lies in the importance attached to freedom of expression. Any constraint of the free circulation of ideas and information obviously entails strong justification.

Political speech attracts special protection.[74] But even gossip has a role in social and political life – unless, of course, it gratuitously disseminates personal information that violates privacy.[75] A 'public figure'[76] does not forfeit all protection; although the suggestion is often made that where he or she is a role model different considerations might apply. But it is hardly 'self-evident', in the words of Lord Woolf, that a famous footballer's activities off the field have 'a modicum of public interest … [because they] are role models for young people and undesirable behaviour on their part can set an unfortunate example'.[77]

It is frequently asserted that since celebrities savour publicity when it is positive, they cannot complain when it is intrusive. The fact that public figures attract – or even court – publicity cannot be permitted to defeat their right to protect intimate features of their lives from public disclosure.[78]

---

[72] ibid, at [24].

[73] American law inclines toward a test of 'newsworthiness' which normally generates a similar set of questions, though it seems needlessly to complicate the matter.

[74] In *Campbell* (n 25 above) Baroness Hale said: 'There are undoubtedly different types of speech, just as there are different types of private information, some of which are more deserving of protection in a democratic society than others. Top of the list is political speech. The free exchange of information and ideas on matters relevant to the organisation of the economic, social and political life of the country is crucial to any democracy. Without this, it can scarcely be called a democracy at all. This includes revealing information about public figures, especially those in elective office, which would otherwise be private but is relevant to their participation in public life', at [148].

[75] See *Couderc and Hachette Filipacchi Associés v France* Application no 40454/07, [2016] EMLR 19 at [123].

[76] The English courts have wrestled with the question of who is a public figure. See, for example, *Campbell* (n 25 above); Cf *McKennitt v Ash* [2007] 3 WLR 194; *A v B* [2002] EWCA Civ 337, [2003] QB 125; *Goodwin v News Group Newspapers Ltd* [2011] EWHC 1437 (QB), [2011] EMLR 27; *Ferdinand v Mirror Group Newspapers Ltd* [2011] EWHC 2454 (QB). See the discussion below of the *Von Hannover* decisions of the Strasbourg Court.

[77] *A v B* [2002] EWCA Civ 337, [2003] QB 195. See too *Hutcheson (formerly known as KGM) v News Group Newspapers Ltd* [2012] EMLR 2; *Steve McClaren v News Group Newspapers Ltd* [2012] EWHC 2466 (QB); *Theakston v Mirror Group Newspapers* [2002] EWHC 137 (QB). See the discussion in R Wacks, *Privacy and Media Freedom*, n 56 above, 152–58.

[78] The Leveson Inquiry found 'ample evidence that parts of the press have taken the view that actors, footballers, writers, pop stars – anyone in whom the public might take an interest – are fair game, public

It is also claimed that the media have the right to 'put the record straight.' So, for example, in the case of supermodel Naomi Campbell, because she had lied about her drug addiction, there was, the Court of Appeal held, a public interest in the press revealing the truth. But suppose a celebrity were suffering from cancer or AIDS, can it really be the case that a reasonable wish to conceal this fact – unless it was directly relevant to their ability to exercise their job, for example – should be overridden by the media's right to 'put the record straight'? If so, the protection of personal information is rendered unduly flimsy.

The nature of the information sought to be protected is an important criterion in the determination of whether protection is warranted. Thus, both the English courts and the EU's recent *Guidelines on Safeguarding Privacy in the Media*[79] recognise that details in an individual's medical or financial records are prima facie private. Beyond that, it is generally accepted that particulars of a person's sexual activity normally warrant protection.[80]

So, for example, in *Mosley v News Group Newspapers*[81] the claimant, President of *Federation Internationale de l'Automobile*, had engaged in sado-masochistic activities which were secretly filmed by one of the participants who gave an interview to a tabloid newspaper which was published under the heading 'F1 Boss has Sick Nazi Orgy with 5 Hookers.' An edited version of the video was uploaded to the tabloid's website. In the space of two days it had been viewed over 1.4 million times while the online version of article had been visited some 400,000 times. The newspaper voluntarily (and swiftly) removed the edited video footage from its website, and agreed not to show the images again without 24 hours' notice.

In regard to Article 8, the High Court acknowledged that in the case of photography, the mere fact of surreptitious recording may be regarded as an intrusion, and an improper violation of Article 8. And it treated the subsequent publication of the material as a separate issue. The newspaper pleaded public interest in disclosure, and that Article 10 ought to prevail. The public interest as originally framed concerned the allegation that the S&M session involved Nazi or concentration camp role-play. This was subsequently widened to include the claim that the acts involved illegality: assault occasioning actual bodily harm and brothel keeping. The public interest, it was argued, related to Mosley being a role model as President of the FIA. On the evidence, the Court found that the S&M session did not involve

---

property with little, if any, entitlement to any sort of private life or respect for dignity, whether or not there is a true public interest in knowing how they spend their lives. Their families, including their children, are pursued and important personal moments are destroyed. Where there is a genuine public interest in what they are doing, that is one thing; too often, there is not.' *An Inquiry into the Culture, Practices and Ethics of the Press*, HC 780 (November 2012), Executive Summary, para 33.

[79] https://rm.coe.int/guidelines-on-safeguarding-privacy-in-the-media-final-r3/168075ac59. The document was formulated by the Council of Europe's *Partnership for Good Governance* 'targeting cooperation activities with Armenia, Azerbaijan, Georgia, the Republic of Moldova, Ukraine and Belarus.'

[80] But compare *A v B* [2002] EWCA Civ 337, [2003] QB 195 and *CC v AB* [2006] EWHC 3083 (QB), 2007 EMLR 20.

[81] *Mosley v News Group Newspapers* [2008] EWHC 1777 (QB), [2008] EMLR 20.

a Nazi theme. It accepted that Mosley's Article 8 rights had been engaged. As to the defendant's rights under Article 10, it was argued that Mosley's behaviour exhibited depravity and adultery; there was therefore a public interest in its disclosure. The judge, Eady J, gave this high-minded contention short shrift:

> The modern approach to personal privacy and to sexual preferences and practices is different from that of past generations. First there is a greater willingness ... to accord respect to an individual's right to conduct his or her personal life without state interference or condemnation. It has to be recognized that sexual conduct is a significant aspect of human life in respect of which people should be free to choose ... It is important in this new rights-based jurisprudence to ensure that where breaches occur remedies are not refused because an individual journalist or judge finds the conduct distasteful or contrary to moral or religious teaching.[82]

The test by which the public interest is to be judged is whether the disclosure makes a genuine contribution to the debate on matters of general interest and not 'vapid tittle-tattle.'[83] This approach has been adopted by the Strasbourg Court in a number of cases involving Princess Caroline of Monaco. Her complaint in one action was that paparazzi employed by several German magazines had photographed her while she was engaged in a variety of quotidian activities, including eating in a restaurant courtyard, horse riding, canoeing, playing with her children, shopping, skiing, kissing a boyfriend, playing tennis, sitting on a beach, and so on. A German court found in her favour in respect of the photographs which, though in a public place, were taken when she had 'sought seclusion'.

But, while accepting that some of the pictures were sufficiently private to merit protection, the court dismissed her complaint in regard to the rest. She appealed to the European Court of Human Rights, which accepted that Article 8 applied, but balanced the protection of her private life against the freedom of expression guaranteed by Article 10. Taking and publishing photographs, it held, was a practice in which the protection of an individual's rights and reputation assumed especial significance as it did not involve the dissemination of 'ideas', but of images containing personal or even intimate 'information' about that individual. Furthermore, pictures published in the tabloid press were frequently taken in an atmosphere of harassment that caused in the subject a strong sense of intrusion or even of persecution.[84]

---

[82] ibid, at [125].

[83] This was Baroness Hale's apposite phrase in *Jameel v Wall Street Journal* [2006] UKHL 44; [2007] 1 AC 359 at [147] in which the House of Lords, reiterated the 'general obligation of the press, media and other publishers to communicate important information upon matters of general public interest and the general right of the public to receive such information', established in *Reynolds v Times Newspapers Ltd* [2001] 2 AC 127; the so-called '*Reynolds* defence'. See too *Flood v Times Newspapers Ltd* [2012] UKSC 11 in which the Supreme Court unanimously supported a robust public interest defence. See below.

[84] *Von Hannover v Germany* Application no 59320/00, [2004] EMLR 379 (ECHR) (2004) 40 EHRR 1.

The crucial element when balancing the protection of private life against freedom of expression, the Court held, was the contribution that the published photographs and articles made to a debate of general interest. The pictures of the Princess were of a purely private nature, taken without her knowledge or consent and, in some instances, in secret. They made no contribution to a debate of public interest since she was not engaged in an official function; the photographs and articles related exclusively to details of her private life. The public had no legitimate interest in knowing the princess's whereabouts or how she behaved in her private life – even in places that could not always be described as secluded. In the same way as there was a commercial interest for the magazines to publish the photographs and articles, those interests had, in the Court's view, to yield to the applicant's right to the effective protection of her private life.

On the other hand, when images of her and her husband on a skiing holiday were published alongside an article regarding the health of her father, Prince Rainier III of Monaco, the Court held they did not violate her privacy. The health of the reigning prince was a subject of general interest, and the media were entitled to report on 'the manner in which the prince's children reconciled their obligations of family solidarity with the legitimate needs of their private life, among which was the desire to go on holiday'.[85]

Where the plaintiff was accused by the media of the murder of the former Swedish Prime Minister, the European Court held that the unsolved murder was a matter of serious public interest.[86] Similarly, the Court held there was a legitimate public interest in revealing that a child had been fathered out of wedlock by Prince Albert II of Monaco.[87] Where a prison refused to allow a television station to interview a convicted murderer, the Court held that this was a matter of public interest and contributed to the debate about the administration of justice.[88] And when a journalist had been fined for defaming a surgeon by alleging that a patient had died as a result of the surgeon's consumption of alcohol, the Court found that relating the experience of the deceased's surviving widower, and questions of patient safety, were matters of public interest.[89] The treatment of animals has also been held to be a matter of public interest and to contribute to public debate.[90]

Is it a matter of public interest to report the fact that a celebrity is suspected of historical sex offences? The BBC obtained information from the police that Sir Cliff Richard, one of Britain's best-known pop stars, had been accused of a sex offence that he allegedly committed in the 1980s. The BBC received a tip-off from

---

[85] *Von Hannover v Germany (No 2)* Applications nos 40660/08 and 60641/08, [2012] ECHR 228 at [49] and [117].
[86] *White v Sweden* Application no 42435/02, [2007] EMLR 1.
[87] *Couderc and Hachette Filipacchi Associés v France* Application no 40454/07, [2016] EMLR 19.
[88] *Schweizerische Radio- und Fernsehgesellschaft SRG v Switzerland* Application no 34124/06 (judgment of 21 June 2012).
[89] *Selistö v Finland* Application no 56767/00 (judgment of 6 November 2004).
[90] *Guseva v Bulgaria* Application no 6987/07 (judgment of 17 February 2015). Cf *Australian Broadcasting Corporation v Lenah Game Meats Pty Ltd* [2001] HCA 63, (2001) 185 ALR 1.

the police that they were about to conduct a search of Sir Cliff's home (he was not present). It broadcast reports of the search, including film taken from a helicopter, which the judge described as 'somewhat sensationalist'. The High Court found in favour of Sir Cliff, awarding him considerable damages for misuse of private information.

The judge observed that 'it is very significant that the publication started with *obviously private and sensitive information*, obtained from someone who, to the knowledge of (the BBC journalist) ought not to have revealed it' (emphasis added).[91] But is it obviously 'private and sensitive information'? Quite apart from whether the publication was in the public interest,[92] or whether the claimant deserved compensation for his considerable distress,[93] the Court's assumption that information that an individual is suspected of a criminal offence is ipso facto private is highly questionable. The judgment contains no fewer than 142 references to 'privacy', yet the judge's supposition drains the concept of its proper meaning when it is invoked in a situation involving an investigation into alleged criminal conduct.

VII. Data Protection

There is a paradox at the heart of data protection regimes. The GDPR adopts an extravagantly broad concept of 'personal data' protection that extends well beyond the concept of privacy. Personal data is defined in Article 4(1) as

> any information relating to an identified or identifiable natural person ('data subject'); an identifiable natural person is one who can be identified, directly or indirectly, in particular by reference to an identifier such as a name, an identification number, location data, an online identifier or to one or more factors specific to the physical, physiological, genetic, mental, economic, cultural or social identity of that natural person.

While this wide definition obviously incorporates information, the obtaining or disclosure of which would constitute an invasion of 'privacy', its breadth neglects this question. As argued in Chapter one, it is chiefly information that is sensitive

---

[91] *Cliff Richard v BBC*, [2018] EWHC 1837 (Ch) at [292].

[92] The swoop on Sir Cliff was made against the background of a number of police investigations of historic child sex abuse under Operation Yewtree. There were several high-profile arrests, charges, and convictions of public figures. The decision has been criticised by the media as a major infringement of freedom of expression; see for example: http://www.newsmediauk.org/Latest/ newspapers-voice-press-freedom-concerns-following-cliff-richard-bbc-ruling.

[93] Could the case have been pleaded as an intentional infliction of emotional distress as formulated in *Wilkinson v Downton* [1897] 2 QB 57? It may require minor relaxation of the requirements. See Lord Hoffmann's dictum in *Hunter v Canary Wharf* [1997] AC 655 at 707. Cf *Wong v Parkside Health NHS Trust* [2001] EWCA Civ 721; *Wainwright v Home Office* [2001] EWCA Civ 2081, [2002] QB 1334 (CA) at [47]–[49] (per Lord Woolf CJ). See R Wacks, *Privacy and Media Freedom* (Oxford: Oxford University Press, 2013) 205–11. Or, if the innuendo discloses false information, in defamation?

or intimate that warrants protection in the name of privacy. And the protection granted by the GDPR is not always and necessarily meant to guarantee it.

Newsgathering naturally involves the collection, processing, and publishing of personal information. Reconciling freedom of information and data protection bristles with problems. As discussed above, the nucleus of current data protection regimes is the requirement of data subject consent, unless legal compliance, contractual agreement or, as specified in recital 47, a legitimate interest justifies the processing. Having to obtain the consent of an individual who is the subject of a news story, especially one that exposes wrongdoing, would sound the death-knell of investigative – and even quotidian – journalism.

Article 85 of the GDPR attempts to resolve this challenge by providing exemptions from some of the data protection principles where processing is conducted in pursuit of 'journalistic purposes'. But even where the journalistic exemption applies, it only exempts the media from certain provisions, and only insofar as those provisions are 'incompatible' with the practice of journalism. Nor does it provide an exemption in respect of the obligation under Article 5(1)(f) (personal data must be processed with appropriate technical and organisational measures to ensure it is processed fairly and lawfully.)

And one might wonder why such a provision has been extended to journalistic activities that are already subjected to a whole set of regulations in relation to the fairness of the reporting, liability for defamation and, in general, responsibilities attaching to broadcasters. At least, this approach recognises that the protection of personal data as such is preferable to focusing on the consequences of their use as an unnecessary duplication. For example, if a broadcaster publishes false personal information about me, it may infringe a code of conduct, but there is no need to invoke the GDPR since I am protected by the law of defamation. Why should it be regarded as a matter of personal data processing? What further protection – and legal remedy – does this sort of provision grant the individual?

The very same question should be asked about non-professional user-generated content. The GDPR does not apply to processing carried out, as Article 2 specifies, 'by a natural person in the course of a purely personal or household activity.' But an individual is still required to abide by the law and by the general principle of 'do no harm'. Why, then, should a professional who shares the identical personal data unlawfully be punished more severely than a private individual who shares the very same personal data in the very same manner?

Three aspects of the GDPR are germane here. First, it is clear that the media are 'data controllers' and therefore subject to its provisions. But, secondly, an exemption is specified in Article 85 in respect of 'journalistic purposes and the purposes of academic, artistic or literary expression.' For processing carried out for journalistic purposes or the purpose of academic artistic or literary expression, Member States are required to provide for exemptions or derogations from various chapters of the Regulation, including Chapter II (principles), Chapter III (rights of the data subject), Chapter IV (controller and processor), Chapter V (transfer of personal data to third countries or international organisations), Chapter VI (independent supervisory authorities), Chapter VII (cooperation and consistency) and Chapter IX (specific data processing situations) if they are necessary to reconcile the right to the protection of personal data with the freedom of expression.

Thirdly, the Regulation provides that personal data which are, by their nature, particularly sensitive in relation to fundamental rights and freedoms merit specific protection as the context of their processing could create significant risks to the fundamental rights and freedoms. Those personal data include personal data revealing racial or ethnic origin, political opinion, religious or philosophical belief, health, sex life, or sexual orientation. Article 9 provides that such data may be processed only where the data subject has consented or him/herself publicises the data, or where it is necessary for public health or archiving in the public interest, scientific, historical research, or statistical purposes.

Most controversially, the GDPR, in addition to the right of access and rectification, incorporates the 'right to erasure'.[94] This questionable concept, widely dubbed the 'right to be forgotten', was recognised by the European Court of Justice in a case in which an individual objected to the results of various searches on the ground that they were no longer relevant. The Court ruled that an Internet search engine operator is accountable for processing of personal data which appear on web pages published by third parties. The judgment was based on Articles 7 and 8 of the Charter of Fundamental Rights which protect respect for private and family life, and the protection of personal data, respectively.[95] But the connection to 'privacy' is tenuous since, by definition, personal information is secret or, at least, non-public, while the right to erasure applies to information that has been publicised.

Article 17 of the GDPR moves the right to be forgotten from a court-created to a provision-backed right, by adopting a prima facie restricted notion. While paragraph 1 and 2 confer the power of data subjects to have their personal data permanently erased as soon as there are neither reasons nor legal requirements for its keeping, paragraph 3 provides an exception for processing that is necessary for the exercise of freedom of expression and freedom of information. It might therefore be argued that there is a distinction between the broad definition of the right to be forgotten devised by the European Court of Justice and the letter of the GDPR's Article 17; some reconciliation between the two, where required, is needed.

Notwithstanding that the two legal categories share the same name ('right to be forgotten') there is an important relevant difference between the two. The ECJ-backed right to be forgotten has a broader reach because it is meant to limit

---

[94] Article 17 obliges data controllers to erase personal data 'without undue delay' when the data is no longer required for the purpose for which it is collected, where an individual objects its being processed, or where the processing is unlawful.
[95] Case C-131/12 *Google Spain SL v Agencia Española de Protección de Datos (AEPD) and Mario Costeja González* [2014] QB 1022. See too *ML and WW v Germany* Application nos 60798/10 and 65599/10, [2018] ECHR 554. While the judgment robustly defends the rights of primary publishers in respect of criminal convictions, the Court stressed that search engine operators do not enjoy the same rights.

the availability of information. It has not been extended, by the Court, to establish a duty to delete the original information, but only the intermediate one (search engine results).[96]

The GDPR right to be forgotten is not, in fact, an actual right to be forgotten – at least not in the sense that is commonly associated with the concept. Article 17 merely says that as soon as there is no reason to process personal data, it must be erased. This is what should happen, for instance, to accounting records whose retention is no longer required by law, expired contracts, outdated versions of currently available information and so on. But it does not extend to limitations of freedom of expression and information.

Actually this distinction does not exist and even if it did, in the practical enforcement of Article 17, it would be of no use to challenge the ECJ's version of the right to be forgotten. Courts are not prevented from entering into the merit of a complaint regarding the right to erasure to see if the freedom of expression and information justification is applicable. Therefore, even under Article 17 a court might declare that a specific item of personal data is no longer relevant to these freedoms, and that, consequently, it should be erased. But as in the case of the legitimacy of public space (candid) photography, the debate cannot be restricted to a contrast between the right to protection of personal data, on the one hand, and the right to freedom of speech and information, on the other.

Preserving information, even the less relevant, and even that related to non-public individuals is a way to preserve the collective memory of a society. Museums are filled with ordinary, quotidian artefacts, scraps of parchment or paper containing shopping lists, trivial agreements, and personal communications. They are an invaluable treasure chest of information that our ancestors left us, and that we are at risk of denying to our descendants.[97]

In short, the right to be forgotten is unrelated to the right to privacy, but if misinterpreted could endanger the ability of posterity to learn how we were.

This is the subject of the next chapter.

---

[96] The legal extension of the right to be forgotten to include search engine indexes by the *Costeja v Google Spain* ECJ decision is unsatisfactory because it is based on the notion that what matters is making information impossible to find, rather than entering into the merits of the infringement of the information itself. This amounts to 'soft' censorship.

[97] Susan Sontag's classic, percipient analysis of photography describes it as predatory: 'To photograph people is to violate them, by seeing them as they never see themselves, by having knowledge of them they can never have; it turns people into objects that can be symbolically possessed. Just as the camera is a sublimation of the gun, to photograph someone is a sublimated murder – a soft murder, appropriate to a sad, frightened time.' *On Photography* (Harmondsworth: Penguin Books, 1977) 14. We beg to differ.

7

Personal Information and Memory

If Lucius Sergius Catilina, the 'Great Conspirator', who in 63 BC attempted to overthrow the Roman Republic, had been given the opportunity to challenge history, he might have asserted his right not to be remembered. This, he would have said, was because the public was no longer interested in him, and he had been depicted in a partisan and unfair manner. Imagine his claim:

> I am Lucius Sergius Catilina, fallen in battle on 5 January 62 BC, in the struggle to free Rome from the claws of a corrupt Senate whose seats were inherited rather than deserved.

> I am Lucius Sergius Catilina, whose noble attempt is still depicted by my former friend and now arch enemy – Marcus Tullius Cicero – as a coup to overthrow the Republic.

> I am Lucius Sergius Catilina and, after more than 2000 years, I deserve to be forgotten.

I. A Right to History

What is the ontological difference between Catilina's claim to be forgotten and that of Mr Costeja's plea to the European Court of Justice to order Google to remove the reports of his past judicial misfortunes? Why should we remember Catilina and not Mr Costeja? How can the Court's decision – ordering the erasure, not of the source of the information, but its concealment – be justified? In the words of the Court:

> [S]ince in the case in point there do not appear to be particular reasons substantiating a preponderant interest of the public in having, in the context of such a search, access to that information … the data subject may, by virtue of Article 12(b) and subparagraph (a) of the first paragraph of Article 14 of Directive 95/46, require those links to be removed from the list of results.[1]

However, that would not be the case if it appeared, for particular reasons, such as the role played by the data subject in public life, that the interference with his

---

[1] Case C-131/12 *Google Spain SL and Google Inc. v Agencia Española de Protección de Datos and Mario Costeja González*, ECLI:EU:C:2014:317, at [98].

fundamental rights was justified by the preponderant interest of the general public in having, on account of its inclusion in the list of results, access to the information in question.[2]

This is a confused finding. It is a consequence of a twofold misunderstanding of what warrants protection by the right to privacy: the overlap between privacy and data protection, and the inadequate attention paid to other individual and collective rights.

Cecily Cardew in Wilde's *The Importance of Being Earnest* declares, 'I keep a diary in order to enter the wonderful secrets of my life.' She rejects her governess's concerns about her revealing possible indiscretions, as well as her subsequent advice to confine them to her memory, by saying that memory 'usually chronicles the things that have never happened and couldn't possibly have happened.'

Access to information from the past, and to personal information in particular, is of fundamental importance not only in respect of official documents, but also private affairs (sometimes personal, sometimes not) that can provide significant insights into 'how we were'. As the French historian, Marc Bloch, puts it in his short essay, *Apologie pour l'histoire*:

> The successive technological revolutions have disproportionately widened the psychological gap between generations. … [T]he man of the age of electricity or of human flight feels very distant from his ancestors. He willingly – though imprudently – concludes that they do not influence him anymore. Furthermore, add the modernist attitude innate to any engineering mentality. To start and repair a dynamo is it necessary to have mastered the ideas of old Volta on galvanism? By an analogy, no doubt lame, but which imposes itself spontaneously on more than one intelligence subjected to the machine, there will also be someone who thinks that, to understand the great human problems of the current times and to try to solve them, it is worth nothing to have analysed their antecedents.[3]

Consider the extraordinary example of the Oyneg Shabes-Ringelblum, a clandestine association which, to ensure the plight and eventual murder of Polish Jews in the Warsaw ghetto would never be forgotten, secretly collected and concealed documents, photographs, personal diaries and other sources of information. Much of this material was 'anodyne' (as a French court might describe it), but the collection is of major historical significance.

Why should we be denied access to, say, the personal diary of one of Sigmund Freud's patients?[4] While it contains intimate personal information, surely it sheds light on how the father of psychoanalysis practised his craft. Similarly, on what grounds should we be denied access to the subjective artistic process that created

---

[2] ibid, at [99].

[3] Marc Bloch, *Apologie pour l'histoire ou le métier de l'historien* (Paris: Librairie Armand Colin, 1949) 9. Translated by Andrea Monti.

[4] Anna Koellreuter, 'Being Analysed by Freud in 1921: The Diary of a Patient' (2008) 9 *Psychoanalysis and History* 137.

great works of art?[5] Apart from their value to a collector, these scraps are a valuable way of penetrating the mind of the artist to understand the creative process.

In short, preserving the memory of the past is not merely a right, but a collective duty. The fact that information is old ought to render it accessible rather than erasable. Timeworn information was once current, and it is precisely the aging process that increases, rather than diminishes, its importance for historians and social scientists. Thus, if we accept that highly sensitive information, such as the diary of one of Freud's patients, can now be published, what principle or policy justifiably dictates that public information relating to Mr Costejas should be made to disappear? The answer is simple: there is neither a principle nor a policy to dictate this outcome. Indeed, this is accepted by the Court which ordered that the search engine results that link to the information be removed, instead of actually requiring its deletion, as would have been logical, following the reasoning of the decision. In other words, the Court retreated from establishing a precedent that publicly available information can and must be erased.

II. Photographs

There is the hidden treasure of historical (personal) information sealed and buried in the analogue repositories of journals, magazines and – more recently – broadcasting corporations' archives. When, more than a century ago, *The New York Times* was founded, several unpublished photographs were, after a few days of ephemeral celebrity, discarded into a basement known as 'The Morgue'. Over time, this archive grew; it became an increasingly difficult task to locate a particular picture. While photographs were archived under various retrieval categories, a journalist in search of a certain image would have to rely upon the skill of the archivist rather than on direct access to the images. In other words, the ability of the journalist to find a specific photograph was enhanced (or hampered) by the choices of the archive-keeper.

To double-check the existence of a specific photograph when the number of the pictures was (relatively) small, a 'brute force' search (combing through the store of images individually) would have been possible. But with a current archive of some seven million images, the most recent, of course, digitally generated and organised, finding a particular photograph, especially ancient ones, is close to impossible. This is extremely frustrating for those who make a living from creating and managing information.

---

[5] Consider the (less grandiose) example of The Beatles' early compositions which are now displayed in the Manuscript Room of the British Museum, thanks to Hunter Davies, official biographer of the group, who collected the scraps of paper containing rough drafts of the raw and unfinished lyrics. See Hunter Davies, 'Beatles lyrics I saved from the bin are my gift to the nation', *Daily Telegraph*, online version, 24 May 2013: https://www.telegraph.co.uk/culture/10078829/Beatles-lyrics-I-saved-from-the-bin-are-my-gift-to-the-nation.html (visited 18 November 2018).

After having considered how best to overcome this problem, on 9 November 2018 the *New York Times* finally announced a joint venture with Google to digitise its whole analogue archive dating back to the nineteenth century:

> The process will uncover some never-before-seen-documents, equip Times journalists with an easily accessible historical reference source, and preserve The Times's history, one of its most unique assets.[6]

The technicalities of this enormous project are interesting,[7] not merely in regard to the process of digitisation. Scanning vast quantities of analogue information to render it searchable is nothing new to Google; it achieved this outcome with its Google Books project that made available and searchable a huge quantity of old and ancient texts submerged in libraries. What is really new in retrieving dead pictures from 'The Morgue' and resuscitating them by way of a powerful software analyser is the possibility it provides to discover new information concealed in the pictures, and establish new connections among people, places and dates:

> Storing the images is only one half of the story. To make an archive like *The Times'* morgue even more accessible and useful, it's beneficial to leverage additional GCP [Google Cloud Platform] features … They can use the Vision API to identify objects, places and images. … Furthermore, AutoML can be used to better identify images in collections using a corpus of already captioned images … The Cloud Natural Language API could be used to add additional semantic information to recognized text.[8]

It is tempting (and not difficult) to imagine an advance in software that would produce an algorithm that can identify the people portrayed in an old photograph, checking their appearance in pictures taken in other places and times, and matching the somatic changes of an individual over time. But is this an issue related to the protection of personal information?

The answer is not straightforward. Although Google's technology appears remarkable, it is still fairly rough; thus this scenario belongs less in a mass-surveillance project than as a plot line in a science fiction novel. The real issue is that the NYT/Google project demonstrates what could occur as a result of a misconceived notion of 'privacy'. The project accesses only objective and non-altered information. One may challenge, for instance, the fact that the photographer failed to shoot the whole scene or that he did not document a particular aspect of an event, or that he chose a specific angle of view to misrepresent a situation. But this does not alter the fact that the photograph nevertheless depicts objective elements. A car is a car, a building is a building, and a face is a face.

---

[6] 'The New York Times Digitizes Millions of Historical Photos Using Google Cloud Technology', *The New York Times* online edition: https://www.nytco.com/new-york-times-google-cloud/ (visited 18 November 2018).
[7] Sam Greenfield, 'Picture what the cloud can do: How the New York Times is using Google Cloud to find untold stories in millions of archived photos': https://cloud.google.com/blog/products/ai-machine-learning/how-the-new-york-times-is-using-google-cloud-to-find-untold-stories-in-millions-of-archived-photos/ (visited 18 November 2018).
[8] Sam Greenfield, ibid.

III. Understanding the Past

In a century or so, however, our online activity will be an important source of information by which to understand contemporary society. It is likely to be a more reliable representation of our real, offline activities. But if our lives are to be whitewashed or airbrushed by the application of the right to be forgotten (or other distorted conceptions of the right to privacy), the role, indeed the responsibility, of historians and social scientists to comprehend and describe how we were will be seriously inhibited.

Nowadays, social scientists often rely upon fragments and tiny objects to explain a fact that happened in the past. But the more society goes digital, the more they will face an entirely different problem: how to evaluate the reliability of the data they unearth. History is frequently not what it seems, and from time to time the declassification of national archives illuminates formerly unknown aspects of specific historical facts or events, or allows a different reading of a previously 'solid' interpretation of a given incident.

A classic example of this problem is the reason that led the *Sant'Uffizio* to accuse Galileo Galilei of heresy. According to the *vulgata* Galileo was tried because of his refusal to accept the Ptolemaic system, favouring instead the Copernican heliocentric system. But in 1983 Professor Pietro Redondi offered a wholly different explanation based on a document discovered in the secret library of the *Sant'Uffizio*, to which he was given access.[9] Redondi showed it was not his endorsement of Copernicus that led to his trial, but his support in his *Il Saggiatore* of the atomic nature of matter; this undermined the Catholic theory of the Eucharist. Prior to his research, the earlier explanation was regarded as incontrovertible. Ten years later, however, another scholar, Professor Mariano Artigas, published a paper based on other previously unknown documents that departed from Redondi's findings while not definitively falsifying his theory.[10] And the story continues.

This is one among many possible examples of the difficulties encountered by social historians. At its heart is the elemental question of how they are to distinguish the truth from fiction when faced with incomplete or contradictory sources. How is it possible to weigh the reliability of an 'outstanding' social network profile which may have been left unattended by its former owner, or of a Wikipedia right-to-be-forgotten 'enhanced' entry? And what of the problems generated by organised disinformation? Are we to treat online-based information as an historical or sociological cul-de-sac?

---

[9] Pietro Redondi, *Galileo eretico*, 1st edn (Turin, Einaudi,1983); 2nd edn (Bari, Laterza, 2009). English translation by Raymond Rosenthal, *Galileo: Heretic* (Princeton NJ: Princeton University Press, 1987).

[10] Mariano Artigas, 'Un nuovo documento sul caso Galileo: EE 291' in *Acta Philosophica* vol 10, fasc. 2 199–214 (Rome: Edizioni Santa Croce, 2001).

IV. Profiling

The question of profiling technologies discussed earlier is applicable in this context. Privacy scholars and advocates are often obsessed by this question. But, as illustrated in Chapter four, politicians, marketers and advertisers expend considerable energy and resources on the raw data they collect in the quest for the perfect recipe to bake those ingredients into a reliable cake of individuals' profiles. Whether they seek to expound the features of the ultimate mass-control society or the timing of the best moment and price to buy or sell an item, their pursuits are mirrored in the academic world with a deluge of researchers seeking public or private grants. These 'individual profiling stakeholders' are interested in methods that eliminate bias, redundancy and inefficiency in online profiling activities and, as a matter of fact, a great deal of research is focused on these aspects.

All things considered, it is not surprising that China takes the lead in this respect. The reading of one among many of the Middle Kingdom's randomly selected studies provides useful insights:

> In this paper, we revisit the problem of Web user profiling in the big data era … We propose a simple but very effective approach for extracting user profile attributes from the Web using big data. To avoid error propagation, the approach processes all the extraction subtasks in one unified model. To further incorporate human knowledge to improve the extraction performance, we propose a Markov logic factor graph (MagicFG) model. The MagicFG model describes human knowledge as first-order logics and combines the logics into the extraction model. Our experiments on a real data set show that the proposed method significantly improves ($+4$–6%; $p \ll 0.01$, t-test) the extraction performance in comparison with several baseline methods.[11]

Leaving aside the mathematical symbols, the goal of these digital fishermen is clear: design a fishnet to throw into a data lake and haul in quarries of the precise size, weight, kind and (political or commercial) taste. An obvious question is whether it is acceptable, for the sake of historical preservation, to allow them to go further in their 'dual-use' research that might weaponise the processing of personal information. Should we restrain them by blocking these fields of scientific investigation?

V. Genetics

The infinite quest for the understanding of mankind is not, however, limited to what we publicly or privately say or do, for there is the prospect of collecting

---

[11] Xiaotao Gu, Hong Yang and Jie Tang, Jing Zhang, 'Web User Profiling using Data Redundancy' in *Proceedings of the 2016 IEEE/ACM International Conference on Advances in Social Networks Analysis and Mining* (San Francisco CA: 2016).

additional information by travelling back in time and space thanks to the achievements of genetics:

> Thirty years ago the first effort was made to reconstruct the history of human differentiation by employing the genetic divergence observed among human groups. The data base comprised gene frequencies, that is, frequencies of alleles at polymorphic loci known to be clearly inherited … There are, however, very few if any data from the past, and stability in time is inferred from the stability in space, essentially the regularity of gene frequency distributions and the very small differences usually observed among populations that live in widely different environments. Fortunately, in very recent times, new developments in molecular technology have generated the hope of obtaining substantial information from individuals or populations that have been dead for a long time.[12]

The contribution of Professor Luigi Luca Cavalli-Sforza, the pioneer in the study of human genetic variation to trace the evolution of mankind, is well captured in the blurb of his *Genes, Peoples and Languages*:[13]

> Luigi Luca Cavalli-Sforza was among the first to ask whether the genes of modern populations contain a historical record of the human species. Cavalli-Sforza and others have answered this question – anticipated by Darwin – with a decisive yes … Cavalli-Sforza raises questions that have serious political, social, and scientific import: When and where did we evolve? How have human societies spread across the continents? How have cultural innovations affected the growth and spread of populations? What is the connection between genes and languages? Always provocative and often astonishing, Cavalli-Sforza explains why there is no genetic basis for racial classification.[14]

But it is not only dead-and-buried creatures that can be restored to life thanks to the advances of science. The convergence of the perseverance of a scientist and the evolution of genetics has created an entirely new field of research to turn our ancestors' mortal vestiges into an invaluable source of information. Yet, as in the case of the complex relationship between profiling techniques and their diverse purposes, mentioned above, once the possibility of ancestor-related genetic screening became available on the market, the situation becomes less than clear.

Services such as *Ancestry.com*, and *23andme.com* both offer, inter alia, genetic health-risk profiling, 'carrier status', and rough DNA phenotyping[15] – analysis of finger length, skin pigmentation, earlobe shape,[16] smell and hair loss – which

---

[12] Luigi Luca Cavalli-Sforza, Paolo Menozzi, Paolo and Alberto Piazza, *The History and Geography of Human Genes*, abridged paperback edition (Princeton NJ: Princeton University Press, 1994) xi.

[13] Luigi Luca Cavalli-Sforza, *Genes, Peoples, and Languages* (Oakland CA: University of California Press, 2001).

[14] https://www.ucpress.edu/book/9780520228733/genes-peoples-and-languages (visited 20 November 2018).

[15] Manfred Kayser, 'Forensic DNA Phenotyping: Predicting human appearance from crime scene material for investigative purposes' (2015) 18 *Forensic Science International* 33; doi: 10.1016/j.fsigen.2015.02.003.

[16] Ancestry.com.

make promises they are unable to keep. The results they offer are based on access-ing different genetic databases containing varied sets of genetic profiling. This affects the overall (statistical) value of the results because of the limited number of individuals whose DNA has been mapped. In other words, the ancestry reports cannot make absolute statements because of the traditional limitations associated with genetic profiling that are well documented in the genetic forensics field. These include the diverse proportion of the ethnicities mapped into national DNA data-bases that might lead to erroneous conclusions in public policy choices.

Furthermore, these companies use statistics to determine their findings while it is still unclear – because of the secrecy of their methods – how their mathematics actually works. According to Professor Jonathan Marks, 'It's all privatized science, and the algorithms are not generally available for peer review.'[17]

For example *23andme.com* traits sample report is replete with elaborate graph-ics, icons and colourful data.[18] But, while the infographics deliver a message of robust reliability, the captions tell another story. Every part of the report that is supposed to answer a question employs phrases such as 'scientists *believe*', 'your genetics make you *unlikely to*', 'this marker is *usually found*' (emphasis added). And the 'fine print' of the *23andme.com* 'Genetic Science' webpage reads:

> The 23andMe PGS test … It is not intended to diagnose any disease. Your ethnicity may affect the relevance of each report and how your genetic health risk results are interpreted. Each genetic health risk report describes if a person has variants associated with a higher risk of developing a disease, but does not describe a person's overall risk of developing the disease. The test is not intended to tell you anything about your current state of health, or to be used to make medical decisions … Our carrier status reports can be used to determine carrier status, but cannot determine if you have two copies of any genetic variant. These carrier reports are not intended to tell you anything about your risk for developing a disease in the future, the health of your fetus, or your newborn child's risk of developing a particular disease later in life.[19]

It is true that this company provides a detailed, comprehensive section on legal information,[20] expressed in comprehensible English, advising potential custom-ers to seek professional counselling before drawing any conclusions from the genetic reports. Nevertheless the fact remains 'their ads always specify that this is for recreational purposes only: lawyer-speak for, "These results have no scientific standing."'[21]

---

[17] Gina Kolata, 'With a Simple DNA Test, Family Histories are Rewritten. Widespread DNA testing has shed light on the ancestry of millions of Americans. But these services have limitations, and the results can be uncertain', *The New York Times*, https://www.nytimes.com/2017/08/28/science/dna-tests-ancestry.html (visited 20 November 2018).

[18] https://permalinks.23andme.com/pdf/samplereport_traits.pdf (visited 20 November 2018).

[19] https://www.23andme.com/genetic-science/ (visited 20 November 2018).

[20] https://www.23andme.com/test-info/ (visited 20 November 2018).

[21] Gina Kolata, n 17 above.

While these companies are paid to facilitate searches of individuals' 'origins' and assist them to find new relatives, they collect huge quantities of bio-samples and genetic profiles that are pertinent to, and useful for, the health and pharmaceutical industry as well as for the companies themselves.

The terms and conditions of *Ancestry.com* state:

> You own your Personal Information … but we need certain rights from you to use that information … By using the Services, you grant us the right to collect, host, transfer, process, analyze, communicate and store your Personal Information (including your Genetic Information) … in order to (a) provide the Services to you and other users, (b) for the purposes described in these Terms and our Privacy Statement, (c) to help our Users discover more about their family histories, and (d) for any other purpose to which you expressly agree, such as sharing with others.[22]

Another American company, *MyHeritage.com*, raises the bar by offering genetic ancestry and phenotype searches, *as well as* access to billions of historical documents. At present, the two types of service (ie the two databases) are not connected but it resembles the situation – and its possible outcomes – of the Google/New York Times 'Morgue' resurrection project.

VI. Privacy

Do these sites raise any privacy issues? It is not easy to tell. In one respect, these recreational services *collect* bio-samples and personal information but provide, as output, rather than additional personal information, statistical trends and generic information that are *related* to personal information. In this regard, they are hardly different from Google, Facebook or LinkedIn, which provide their clients with a subset of information about people, while keeping the much larger part for themselves. On the other hand, taken as a whole, the amount of information (some of a personal nature, some, in the language of the French Supreme Court 'anodyne') can shape a research project, the private needs of companies, and political decisions.

In fact, there is a crossroads where different industrial sectors, political needs and individual expectations intersect. It amounts to a global interconnection of information to use the past to predict the future. Whether this is a viable goal is speculative, but to an overwhelming number of people this is irrelevant; as is whether information and the related inferences are true, false or somewhere in between. All that matters is 'the promise' or, in more mundane terms, the unique selling point, of being free from the deadly stranglehold of *Moira* and *Tychē*.

And to honour this promise, at this crossroads a deal with the Devil is ready to be sealed – an unholy alliance between the collective right to understand the past, on the one hand, and the very particular interests of the (political and commercial)

---

[22] https://www.ancestry.com/cs/legal/termsandconditions (visited 20 November 2018).

powers-that-be, celebrated on the altar of the global information interconnection. A ruthless pragmatism might dictate that the pendulum should swing toward striking the deal, while an individual rights-based approach might require limiting the relentless pursuit of personal information, even for research or historical purposes.

Whatever the choice made, it is plain that the concept of privacy is unsuited to the task. This reality points to a conception of privacy not as opposed to other rights, but as a continuum. Where the right to privacy is inappropriate as a remedy, other individual rights are available to the individual. Whatever the choice, it is plain that invoking the right of privacy is not the soundest solution. In particular, this matter calls for a meticulous recognition of the reliability of the information to avoid revising the past, manipulating the present, and engendering a jaundiced future.

8

Privacy Reconsidered

We exist in two domains: the public and the private. The latter includes intimate or sensitive particulars that we wish to keep to ourselves or share with selected others. The unsolicited exposure of these facts is usually hurtful. We are increasingly vulnerable to these infringements, which may cause severe psychological harm. It is in this violation that the individual's grievance lies: the unauthorised acquisition, use, or disclosure of information that was believed to be private. The moral turpitude of these activities ought to be the starting point of our analysis of the right to privacy.

The literature on privacy abounds with explorations of the functions of privacy; little attention is paid to the wrongness of infractions. Both the pursuit of 'neutral' or 'contextual' models of privacy and the tireless quest for its defining characteristics often eviscerate the concept of its moral content. Lost in the maze of analytical confusion is the core value that is affronted when information that we believed to be personal is obtained or used without our consent.

It is this injustice that the individual looks to the law to prevent or remedy. And the law requires clarity if it is to translate moral outrage into effective protection.

At the heart of our concern is the right to control personal information. The eavesdropper violates our privacy by his acquisition of information about us.[1] The disclosure or publication of this material is, a fortiori, injurious.

In respect of the dissemination of facts, it is worth noting that when the information is false, liability for defamation may arise. In such a case, the law considers whether the victim has suffered damage to his or her reputation. The law has a reasonably well-defined notion of what is to be understood by this form of injury.[2] Equally, by accepting that an invasion of privacy consists in the misuse of personal information, the fundamental wrong that warrants legal recognition is simplified.[3]

Nothing in the preceding pages is intended to diminish or weaken this legal protection. On the contrary, the argument presented here is founded on the

---

[1] Interestingly, in his analysis of 'shame', Sartre provides the example of an eavesdropper who is apprehended in the course of his spying: Jean-Paul Sartre, *Being and Nothingness*, HE Barnes (tr) (London: Routledge, 1969) 259–60.

[2] See generally, R Post, 'The Social Foundation of Defamation Law: Reputation and the Constitution' (1986) 74 *California Law Review* 691.

[3] The distinction between defamation and infringements of the right to privacy has unfortunately been clouded in recent interpretations of Article 8 of the ECHR by the European Court of Human Rights. See Chapter 6 of this volume.

conviction that this fundamental right is most effectively safeguarded by recognition of its core interest: the security of our personal information.

There is a widespread and understandable desire to expand the scope of human rights. In the case of privacy, this, as demonstrated in previous chapters stretches the concept close to breaking point. 'We cannot', it has been justly claimed, 'inflate the concept of human rights so much that it covers the whole realm of justice. Human rights would lose their distinctive moral force.'[4]

This disquieting conceptual amplification of privacy was identified almost four decades ago:

> 'Privacy' has grown into a large and unwieldy concept. Synonymous with autonomy, it has colonized traditional liberties, become entangled with confidentiality, secrecy, defamation, property, and the storage of information. It would be unreasonable to expect a notion as complex as 'privacy' not to spill into regions with which it is closely related, but this process has resulted in the dilution of 'privacy' itself, diminishing the prospect of its own protection as well as the protection of the related interests. In this attenuated, confused and overworked condition, 'privacy' seems beyond redemption …'Privacy' has become as nebulous a concept as 'happiness' or 'security'. Except as a general abstraction of an underlying value, it should not be used as a means to describe a legal right or cause of action.[5]

Instead, it was insisted, the law ought to identify, as the nucleus of the right to privacy, the protection of personal information. And this, it hardly requires, restating, was brought strikingly home by the advent of the Internet and the manifold threats to privacy that it has spawned.

Both the fuzziness of the concept of privacy and the increasingly woolly borders of the right to privacy (drawn especially by the European Court of Human Rights) endanger the viability of the right. And its expansion undermines the (often competing) rights of free speech, security, and the administration of criminal justice. The effect upon associated or rival rights is an often neglected consequence of the vagueness of notion. It is well expressed by Black J (dissenting) in a leading US Supreme Court privacy decision:

> One of the most effective ways of diluting or expanding a constitutionally guaranteed right is to substitute for the crucial word or words of a constitutional guarantee another word or words more or less flexible and more or less restricted in meaning. This fact is well illustrated by the use of the term 'right of privacy' as a comprehensive substitute

---

[4] G Letsas, *A Theory of Interpretation of the European Convention on Human Rights* (Oxford: Oxford University Press, 2007) 25. 'The term "human right" is nearly criterionless. There are unusually few criteria for determining when the term is used correctly and when incorrectly – not just among politicians, but among philosophers, political theorists, and jurisprudents as well. The language of human rights has, in this way, become debased.' James Griffin, *On Human Rights* (Oxford: Oxford University Press, 2008) 14–15.

[5] Raymond Wacks 'The Poverty of "Privacy"' (1980) 96 *Law Quarterly Review* 73, 89, reproduced in R Wacks, *Law, Morality, and the Private Domain* (Hong Kong: Hong Kong University Press, 2000) chapter 7.

for the Fourth Amendment's guarantee against 'unreasonable searches and seizures.' 'Privacy' is a broad, abstract and ambiguous concept which can easily be shrunken in meaning but which can also, on the other hand, easily be interpreted as a constitutional ban against many things other than searches and seizures. I like my privacy as well as the next one, but I am nevertheless compelled to admit that government has a right to invade it unless prohibited by some specific constitutional provision.[6]

This ambiguity and incoherence is best overcome by explicit legislation that treats the protection of personal information as the central concern of the law. A draft Bill along these lines may be found in the Appendix. Although couched in the accepted style of an English common law statute, the text may be enacted, mutatis mutandis, in any jurisdiction.

There is, regrettably, little evidence of a decline in devotion to the 'right to be let alone'. Recently, the Constitutional Court of South Africa, in a comprehensive judgment, held that, in the words of Zondo ACJ, 'the right to privacy entitles an adult person to use or cultivate or possess cannabis in private for his or her personal consumption.' The learned judge added that 'to the extent that the impugned provisions criminalise such cultivation, possession or use of cannabis, they limit the right to privacy.' This right is affirmed in Section 14 of the South African Constitution which provides:

Everyone has the right to privacy, which includes the right not to have–

(a)   their person or home searched;
(b)   their property searched;
(c)   their possessions seized; or
(d)   the privacy of their communications infringed.

This is an infelicitous formulation; it not only frames the 'right to privacy' – a positive right – in negative terms; it is content to offer four examples which the right 'includes'. And these are unhelpfully vague, and, in respect of (d), tautologous.

While this indifferently drafted section itself does not explicitly protect the private use of cannabis, the Court could be forgiven for construing its general purpose to extend to such conduct. Less justifiable, however, is its analysis of the right to privacy itself.[7] Yet again there is a failure to identify the central problem that lies at the core of the concept of privacy. The decision endorses the nebulous Warren and Brandeis notion of privacy criticised in these pages.

In any event, the matter might, as submitted by counsel, have been decided more simply on the basis of the infringement of other rights or liberties entrenched in the Constitution, including equality and human dignity. The Court was unpersuaded.[8]

---

[6] *Griswold v Connecticut* 381 US 479 (1965) at 508.
[7] *Minister of Justice and Constitutional Development and Others v Prince* [2018] ZACC 30: http://www.saflii.org/za/cases/ZACC/2018/30.html.
[8] ibid, at [95]–[96].

The case illustrates the common inclination to assume that threats of state intervention into private life automatically endanger individuals' 'privacy'. This assumption typically rests on a simplistic, undifferentiated concept of privacy in an indiscriminate, colloquial sense. It is employed in a manner similar to that in which 'security' or 'safety' or even 'happiness' might be used to describe a condition or interest. Little or no attempt is made to examine the actual substance of the concept; it is simply presumed that 'privacy' is sufficiently well understood to obviate the need for a rigorous enquiry into its content. Eventually it is so diluted that its utility as a legal right is undermined in a miasma of confusion and incoherence.

When we retain personal information, or share it with others in an unstable or unsafe manner, there is neither memory nor proof of the existence of the facts concerned. When, by contrast we choose to reveal our inner self by carving personal information on a (digital) stone, we must accept that we relinquish the possibility to exert control over it, even if we still maintain formally the legal right to do so. Nevertheless, our legitimate expectation is that we should not, as a result of the use, or misuse, of the information, be subject to discrimination or harassment, or be judged on the basis of what we have revealed or disclosed. When we lose control over personal information there is no practicable means to recover it. While we do, of course, have the right to control personal information, once we voluntarily share it, we lose the control over its subsequent use.

This reality points to a conception of privacy not as opposed to other rights or as a parasitical right, but as a continuum. Where the right to privacy is no longer an effective remedy, other individual rights are available to the individual.

We cannot presume that our personal information is secure from prying or publicity. Our safety online is susceptible to a vast array of assaults. On its own the law is an imperfect guardian of security and confidentiality; technology and precaution are essential aids in the defence of these rights. But, in order for the law to provide the effective tools of prevention and redress, it is vital that it eschews the vagueness of current conceptions of privacy and recognises – ideally by statute – the necessity of identifying and protecting personal information.

Warren and Brandeis' 'right to be alone' may have been appropriate when life was simpler, and information played a significantly less important role than it does today. The idea of living in seclusion is incongruous in a world of social media and transparency. While there is clearly no perfect solution to the challenges described in this book, the model we propose is most likely to afford the essential safeguards that are so desperately needed. This is best achieved by adopting legislative and/or constitutional provisions that explicitly define the right to privacy as the right to control personal information.

APPENDIX

Protection of Privacy Bill[1]

CONTENTS

A

BILL

TO

Protect the right to privacy

BE IT ENACTED by the Queen's most Excellent Majesty, by and with the advice and consent of the Lords Spiritual and Temporal, and Commons, in this present Parliament assembled, and by the authority of the same, as follows:—

1. Personal information

'Personal information' means those facts, communications, or opinions which relate to an individual and which it would be reasonable to that individual to

---

[1] This draft, an earlier version of which was published in R Wacks, *Privacy and Media Freedom* (Oxford: Oxford University Press, 2013), is based on several of the recommendations of the Law Reform Commission of Hong Kong's report, *Civil Liability for Invasion of Privacy*, 2004. The text of this later draft greatly benefited from the perceptive comments of Professor Megan Richardson and Joshua Rozenberg QC whose advice is greatly appreciated; they do not, of course, bear any responsibility for its remaining shortcomings. If enacted, a statute such as this would fall to be interpreted, as s 3(1) of

regard as intimate or sensitive and therefore to want to withhold, or at least to restrict, its collection, use, or publication.

2. Intrusion

(1) Any person who intentionally obtains personal information relating to another ('the claimant') against the will of that other and/or in circumstances where that other loses control over the aforementioned personal information as a consequence of the intrusion should be liable in tort, provided that the intrusion is highly offensive to a reasonable person of ordinary sensibilities.

(2) A court shall take into account the following factors when determining whether the intrusion constitutes a tort:

   (a) the place where the intrusion occurred (for example, whether the claimant is at home, in office premises or in a public place, and whether or not the place is open to public view from a place accessible to the public, or whether or not the conversation is audible to passers-by);

   (b) the object and occasion of the intrusion; and

   (c) the means of intrusion employed and the nature of any device used (for example, whether the intrusion is effected by means of a high-technology sense-enhancing device, or by mere observation or natural hearing).

Highly offensive

(3) A court shall take into account the following factors when determining whether an intrusion was highly offensive to a reasonable person:

   (a) the extent and duration of the intrusion;

   (b) the means by which the intrusion was conducted;

   (c) the type of information obtained or sought to be obtained by means of the intrusion;

   (d) whether the claimant could reasonably expect to be free from such conduct in the location where it was carried out;

   (e) whether the claimant has taken any steps which would indicate to a reasonable person the claimant's desire that the defendant not engage in the intrusive conduct.

Defences

(4) The following are defences to an action for intrusion:

   (a) the claimant expressly or by implication authorised or consented to the intrusion;

---

the Human Rights Act 1998 requires, in a manner that conforms to the ECHR: 'So far as it is possible to do so, primary and subordinate legislation must be read and given effect in a way which is compatible with the Convention rights.' This should not give rise to any difficulties in respect of the rights protected under Article 8 and Article 10 with which it is generally consistent. Although drafted in common law style, this Bill could, of course, be adapted to civil law systems.

(b) the act or conduct in question was authorised by or under any enactment or rule of law;

(c) the intrusion has been authorised by or under any enactment or rule of law;

(d) the act or conduct constituting the intrusion was necessary for and proportionate to:

(i) the protection of the person or property of the defendant or another;

(ii) the prevention, detection or investigation of crime;

(iii) the prevention, preclusion or redress of unlawful or seriously improper conduct;

(iv) the protection of national security.

3. Public disclosure of personal information

(1) Any person who gives publicity to personal information relating to another should be liable in tort provided that the publicity is of a kind that would be highly offensive to a reasonable person of ordinary sensibilities and he or she knows or ought to know in all the circumstances that the publicity would be highly offensive to such a person.

Highly offensive

(2) A court shall take into account the following factors when determining whether the publicity would be highly offensive to a reasonable person:

(a) whether the facts, communications, or opinions, pertaining to an individual are particularly sensitive or intimate;

(b) whether the defendant used unlawful or intrusive means to obtain the facts, communications or opinions;

(c) the manner of publication;

(d) the extent of the dissemination;

(e) the degree of harm to the claimant's legitimate interests; and

(f) the motive of the defendant.

Defences

(1) The following are defences to an action for public disclosure:

(a) the claimant has expressly or by implication authorised or consented to the publication;

(b) the publicity has been authorised by or under any enactment or rule of law;

(c) the publicity would have been privileged had the action been for defamation;

(d) the publication was in the public interest.

4. Public interest

(1)   A court shall take into account the following questions when determining whether the publicity was in the public interest:

    (a) To whom was the information given?
    (b) Is the claimant a public figure?
    (c) Was the claimant in a public place?
    (d) Is the information in the public domain?
    (e) How was the information acquired?
    (f) What was the defendant's motive?
    (g) Was it essential for the claimant's identity to be revealed?

(2)   The publication should be rebuttably presumed to be in the public interest if it was necessary for:

    (a) the prevention, detection, or investigation of crime;
    (b) the prevention of unlawful or seriously improper conduct;
    (c) establishing whether the claimant was able to discharge his or her public or professional obligations;
    (d) establishing whether the claimant was fit for any public office or profession held or carried on by him or her, or which he or she sought to hold or carry on;
    (e) the prevention of the public being materially misled by a public statement made by the claimant;
    (f) the protection of public health or safety;
    (g) the protection of national security,

and was proportionate to the legitimate aims pursued by the defendant.

(3)   The claimant should not be precluded from obtaining relief by reason merely of the fact that the matter to which the defendant has allegedly given publicity:

    (a) could be found in a register to which the public or a section of the public had access;
    (b) has been disclosed by the claimant to his or her family members, friends, or other individuals;
    (c) has been disclosed or published by a third party without the consent of the claimant;
    (d) has been posted on the Internet by a third party without the consent of the claimant; or
    (e) related to an event which occurred in a place visible or accessible to the public.

5. Remedies

(1)   In an action for intrusion or public disclosure of personal information a court may:

    (a) award damages, including, where appropriate, exemplary damages;

(b) grant an injunction if it shall appear just and convenient;

(c) order the defendant to account to the claimant for any profits which he has made by reason or in consequence of the intrusion or unwarranted publicity; or order the defendant to destroy or deliver up to the claimant any articles or documents containing information about the claimant which have come into the possession of the defendant by reason or in consequence of the intrusion or, as the case may be, which have resulted in the defendant being held liable to the claimant for public disclosure of personal information.

(2) Damages shall include compensation/damages for injury to feelings.

(3) In awarding damages a court shall have regard to all the circumstances of the case, including:

(a) the effect of the intrusion or disclosure of personal information on the health, welfare, social, business or financial position of the claimant or his or her family;

(b) any distress, annoyance, embarrassment or humiliation suffered by the claimant or his or her family; and

(c) the conduct of the claimant and the defendant both before and after the intrusion or disclosure, including publicity for, and the adequacy and manner of, any apology or offer of amends made by the defendant.

6. Hearing

(1) A hearing in an action for intrusion or disclosure may be held in private if publicity would defeat the object of the hearing.

(2) The court may order that the identity of any party or witness shall not be disclosed if it considers non-disclosure necessary in order to protect the interests of that party or witness.

7. Living individuals

Actions for intrusion or unwarranted publicity should be limited to actions against living individuals and the person to whom any right of action should accrue is the individual whose right to privacy is threatened or has been infringed.

8. Operators of websites

(1) This section applies where an action for disclosure of personal information is brought against the operator of a website in respect of a statement posted on the website.

(2) It is a defence for the operator to show that it was not the operator who posted the statement on the website.

(3) The defence is defeated if the claimant shows that—

(a) it was not possible for the claimant to identify the person who posted the statement,

(b) the claimant gave the operator a notice of complaint in relation to the statement, and

(c) the operator failed to respond to the notice of complaint.

(4) For the purposes of subsection (3)(a), it is possible for a claimant to 'identify' a person only if the claimant has sufficient information to bring proceedings against the person.

9. Order for removal of publication from website

(1) Where a court gives judgment for the claimant the court may order the operator of a website on which the publication of personal information is posted to remove the statement.

(2) Subsection (1) does not affect any other power of the court in respect of the publication.

****

INDEX

Note: Alphabetical arrangement is word-by-word, where a group of letters followed by a space is filed before the same group of letters followed by a letter, eg 'art works' will appear before 'artificial intelligence'. In determining alphabetical arrangement, initial articles and prepositions are ignored.

inefficiency:
elimination, profiling, 120
information:
anodyne, 101, 116, 123
clinical, patients, 85
cultural factors, 16
currently available, outdated versions, 114
DNA, extracted from, 84
as fact, 86
fair practice, 20
freedom of, *see* freedom of information
generic, *see* generic information
global interconnection of, using past to
    predict future, 123–24
individual:
    generated by personal computers and
        smartphones, 46
    shares, information professionals and,
        distinction between, 94
intimate, 64
known about individuals, 9
medical, *see* medical information
obtaining constituting invasion of privacy,
    111
from past, access to, 116
photographs as carriers of, 96
physical, profiling, 55
preserving:
    collective memory of society, 114
private:
    about citizens, collecting and organising,
        37
    misuse, 10
    profiling, 55
    use, 10
psychographic-oriented, 56
psychological, 55
public:
    about citizens, collecting and organising,
        37
    creative use, 40
    on personal matters, collecting, 39
    subtle use, 40
publicised by individuals on networked user-
    generated content platforms, 95
publicised by individuals on social
    networking, 95
publicly available but re-shared, 95
publicly shared by owners, 95
rights:
    freedom of, 94
self-shared in social networking, 40–41

software extracting or enhancing, 102
storage, *see* storage of information
technology, *see* information technology
terminal equipment, stored in, EU, 27
users, *see* users
information commissioners:
data protection policy formation by, 21
privacy policy formation by, 21
information professionals:
individual information shares and,
    distinction between, 94
**Information Providers Guide, European
    Commission,** 28
information technology:
mass surveillance using, 37
informational privacy, 41, 42
informational self-determination, 19
**informational technology systems,
    Germany,** 4
informed consent:
data subjects, 85
genetic research, 84
infringement:
claims, rights to privacy, 101
of privacy theory, 17–18
secrecy of communication, 49
injunctions, interim, 91
innovation:
protection, 54
instantaneous threats:
data protection, 21
integrity:
data, EU, 22
personal data, 25
physical, *see* physical integrity
psychological, privacy construed as, 3
intellectual property:
protection, 52
see also copyright
intelligence:
artificial, 57
domestic, 37
governments, 35
Open Source Intelligence, 39
telephone records analysis, 46
interconnected world, 61
interest base of common law, 13
interests:
market, *see* market interests
privacy as amorphous cluster of, 90
interference, privacy, 17
interim injunctions, 91

www.ingramcontent.com/pod-product-compliance
Lightning Source LLC
Chambersburg PA
CBHW061312220326
41599CB00026B/4847